# Contents

# TEACHERS' NOTES

In writing this book for GCSE: Design and Communication, I have tried to satisfy the essence of the course as well as to cover most of the contents of the syllabus. Certain things in this book don't appear in any of the syllabuses, however, and there are some syllabus areas that I've had to leave out (mostly in the geometry area) in order to keep the book to a reasonable size. My aim was to avoid confusion and to allow students of wide-ranging abilities to focus on particular design skills as and when they tackle the projects. This is what makes this course and book different from other graphical communication books but very similar to those about design and technology.

This book emphasises, and is based on, three important principles:

1. That design and communication is a designing activity.
2. That designing has to be a people-centred activity. (The projects are all intended for a client, that is the person whom the work is being done for.)
3. That the students should have as much control over their learning as possible.

The book contains a number of projects within which the teacher can weave the content items of the syllabus. As mentioned above, it will be of great value to the students if they can aim their projects at a real 'client', i.e. someone whom they know, such as a parent, friend, teacher, other students etc., who can role play the client. Their existence makes more meaningful the concept of design and communication. (If this is not possible, students can imagine the client.) The projects are presented in a more or less logical order, though the teacher is free to vary the order and modify the projects to suit their students' needs.

Crucial to the success of the course are:

1. Discussion and negotiation.
2. Presentation and storage of students' work.
3. Recording of progress.
4. Expansion of the kind of activities that go on.

Throughout the book there is a lot of emphasis on working with other people, discussing and negotiating with teachers and fellow students, and giving support and criticism. This is because designing and communicating involve people, and it is essential that students are actively involved in explaining and justifying their work at all levels. Not all the students will be familiar with this approach. Several of the projects and topics involve tests and games which involve two people working together. It works best when both students have information that they can pool and then produce the solution together.

The skills involved in working in groups are listening, thinking about yourself and the effect you have on others, and joining in. These skills can be practised separately but they are most effective when practised together. The following idea takes time but is valuable as a learning strategy. At the start and finish of each session small groups can sit around a table or in a circle to plan or review their progress. The opinions of each student should be heard in turn, with a spokesperson representing opinions back to the whole group. The teacher can keep records on each group and encourage the students to fill in their self evaluation sheets (see Project 1) with what the group has done as well as what they have done individually.

One exercise to encourage listening skills is to form groups and get each student to say something that is personal to them, like: 'What I am going to try to do in this session is…'. In turn, each student has to repeat what the previous student has said before stating their own objective. The last student repeats from memory what everyone in the group has said. This can be intimidating until the students realise that they can prompt each other, and it does encourage them to listen to what others are saying.

All the projects emphasise the good presentation of work. Encourage the students to collect a portfolio of their best work and compile a profile of positive achievements (see Projects 2 and 3). These will help to build a student's confidence and also encourage respect of each other's abilities.

The facilities in the area or room used for the course may need to be rearranged so that the course can operate successfully.

# Design and Technology and the National Curriculum

The subject covered by this book fits within the Design and Technology component of the National Curriculum. With the emphasis on project work, the variety of related activities concentrate on the 'processes' of identifying needs, designing, planning and making, and appraising. This is echoed by the proposals for the National Curriculum in Design and Technology as stated in Attainment Targets 1 to 4.

This book will provide valuable experience and starting points for collaboration and cooperation, as teachers began to implement the National Curriculum, during the transition to Design and Technology from what are now separate subject areas (CDT, Home Economics, Business Studies, Art and Design, Information Technology).

Whilst centred around Design and Communication the framework should help both students and teachers, working through projects to maintain both relevance and rigour, matching syllabus content with involvement and motivation.

*August 1989*

# Self Evaluation Sheet

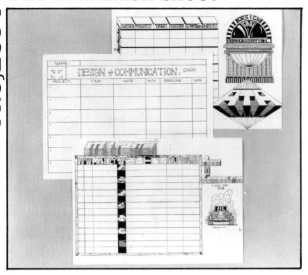

This book is divided into two sections – projects and skills. You will cover the skills as and when you need them for the project work. What you also have to do is to find a way of saying what you have done lesson by lesson and then, at certain times, you should look back and record the topics you have covered. The ways I suggest you do this I have called self evaluation sheets, end statements and course profiles.

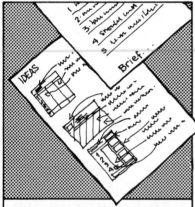

WRITE OUT THE BRIEF AND ANY IDEAS YOU HAVE FOR YOUR EVALUATION SHEET.

DISCUSS YOUR IDEAS WITH SOMEONE ELSE, WRITE DOWN ANY NEW IDEAS.

A self evaluation sheet should have spaces for:
- your name;
- the dates that it covers;
- what you did in the lesson;
- comments as to how well you worked;
- teacher's comments;
- reminders and notes for the next lesson;
- homework topics;
- parents' comments;
- general information.

When you have worked out what has to go on to your self evaluation sheet see if you can come up with several different ideas for its design. Try drawing them out and filling them in to see if they work. When you have an idea that you are happy with, draw it out neatly.

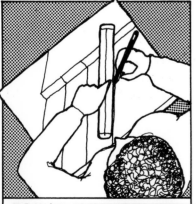

DRAW OUT THE IDEA YOU LIKE, TRY FILLING IT IN, CHANGE IT IF NECESSARY.

FINALLY DRAW OUT THE IMPROVED VERSION OF YOUR IDEA, WITH CARE!

# Self Evaluation Sheet

Discuss your design ideas with someone, listen carefully to their comments and try to bring these ideas into your design.

Design yourself a logo to go on your work. Try out several ideas, choose the best one, draw it out and paste it in place.

You may want to duplicate self evaluation sheets or you may feel that it is better that you design one, try it out and then modify it.

DISCUSS YOUR LAYOUT IDEA, WORK OUT THE WORDS YOU NEED ON IT.

PRODUCE A BRIEF AND IDEAS FOR A LOGO. LOOK AT EXISTING LOGOS.

CHOOSE THE DESIGN FOR YOUR LOGO AND CHECK THE SPACE AVAILABLE.

SCALE DOWN THE LOGO TO FIT THE SPACE YOU HAVE LEFT FOR IT.

CHOOSE THE STYLE AND SIZE OF LETTERING YOU WANT ON YOUR SHEET.

CAREFULLY 'PASTE' ALL OF THE PIECES INTO PLACE.

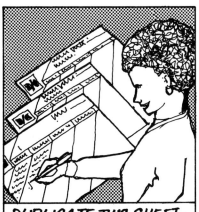

DUPLICATE THIS SHEET - USE IT TO PLAN AND TO RECORD THE WORK DONE

## References

# End Statements

Saying how well you have done things can be difficult. The idea is to record things that you can do, and particularly things that you can do well.

**Teacher's note**   It may be useful if, rather than asking students to write out what they have covered, they are given a list of possible topics for each project and then asked to record only the ones covered. This should leave you in the position of being able to negotiate with the individual student as to what they have covered and how well.

6. CAN PRODUCE A PERSONAL LOGO

7 CAN PRODUCE A SELF EVALUATION SHEET

CUT HERE.

8. CAN TAKE 'RECORD' PHOTOGRAPHS

9. CAN WRITE A LETTER OF INTRODUCTION

10. CAN WRITE A LETTER GIVING PERMISSION

11. CAN PRODUCE A 'ROUGH' PLAN VIEW FROM MEASUREMENTS.

12. CAN PRODUCE A DETAILED PLAN

## Brief

Design a way of saying what you can do at the end of a project. In the example above there are two things that you can now do after designing and producing a self evaluation sheet.

PRODUCE A LIST OF THE THINGS THAT YOU'VE COVERED IN THE PROJECT.

DISCUSS THESE WITH YOUR TEACHER. HOW 'WELL' CAN YOU DO THEM?

Much of the current thinking about course structure and assessment is very similar to this approach. It will fit in well with CPVE profiling and BTec courses as well as with GCSE.

FINALLY PASTE UP AN 'END STATEMENT' WHICH SAYS WHAT YOU CAN DO.

## References

# Course Profile

**Teachers' note**   It is possible to lay out the course as a series of syllabus items that should be covered. The chart below is based on the LEAG syllabus. As you can see, it is a bit complicated and you may find that it is more sensible to introduce this sometime after the course has started and to concentrate initially on end statements.

As the project work progresses, the students should be able to see which areas they have covered and also which ones they still have to cover. The idea is that the students progress from a basic recording of what they have done to an awareness of what this means as far as the whole course is concerned. The suggestion is that you **focus** their achievements by using end statements.

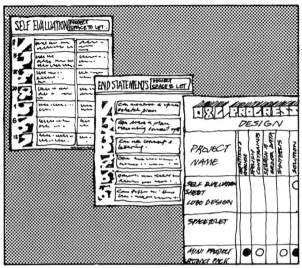

One of the most difficult things about relating a whole course to a chart, is that areas covered come in a variety of levels.

- Skills – like instrument drawing.
- Groups of skills – like engineering drawing.
- Attitudes – like the way that graphics and the needs of people relate to each other.

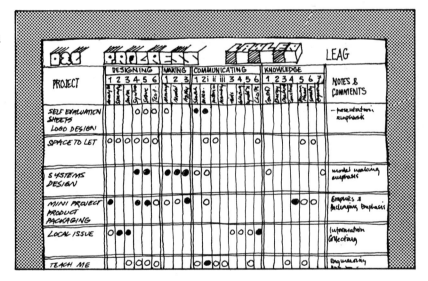

## References

# Space To Let

PROJECT 4

The purpose of this project is to describe a space (a room, or a building) to someone else, using the most suitable graphical way of doing so.

Choose a client (real or imaginary) who wants to use this space. It could be the corner of a park where the client wants to set up a children's playground; it could be a room where the client wants to hold dancing lessons, or a public meeting, or a party. You might decide that you are an estate agent who is about to sell a house.

Often the hardest decision will be which space to choose. It is better to pick somewhere that you can get to easily and often, even though it may be less exciting.

You now have to decide **what** information you need e.g. what does the client want to do in this space? This may mean you have to go and talk to the 'client', or perhaps just imagine what will be needed. At this point you will probably have some idea of both **how** and **what** you will eventually do. Don't forget to make a note of these ideas, but resist the temptation to rush into a final answer.

Decide on the best way to collect the information you need. At this point it may mean doing some guessing, but you can always go back and find out the things you've missed as you go along.

You will need to go and look at the space. This may mean that you have to get permission to be there, plus a letter of introduction. Include these in your project presentation.

Measure and sketch or photograph the space, and discuss it with your client.

COLLECT INFORMATION ABOUT YOUR 'SPACE' INTERVIEWS, PHOTOS ETC.

ASK YOUR 'CLIENT' WHAT THEY WILL NEED IN THE SPACE.

MEASURE, SKETCH, DRAW PLANS. HAVE YOU MISSED ANYTHING?

DISCUSS WHAT YOU HAVE DONE SO FAR, LISTEN AND MAKE NOTES.

# Space To Let

Now the difficult part – deciding **what** to present and **how** to present it. This may mean producing several ideas or sketch versions of your ideas (these are often called 'roughs' but it still means you have to do them carefully). Judge which of them is the best or maybe the easiest for you to produce a good result. Make a note of your reasons for choosing the one you do.

Very carefully put together your chosen idea. Try to work out the overall layout in detail first. Think ahead and try to avoid things where a slip or mistake can ruin the whole thing (see paste-up, page 47).

You should now have a series of pieces of work which describe your chosen space. These may be drawings, text, photographs, posters, models or whatever you have chosen to do.

Now to assess how well the things work. Obviously your 'client' can not only give advice but may also be able to give constructive comments about your work. Check that you have used the correct standards for written and drawn parts of your work. (Is the spelling correct? Have you used the correct symbols for building drawing?)

LOOK AT THE MATERIAL YOU HAVE COLLECTED. HOW SHOULD IT BE PRESENTED?

WHAT ARE THE POSSIBLE METHODS? POSTER, BOOKLET, MODEL?

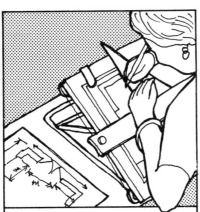

WORK OUT THE LAYOUT. DRAW OUT THE PIECES OF YOUR PRESENTATION.

PUT UP A DISPLAY OF YOUR WORK. EXPLAIN WHAT YOU HAVE DONE.

DISCUSS YOUR WORK WITH THE 'CLIENT'. MAKE NOTES OF ANY COMMENTS.

Make a record of your own feelings about the project, particularly the things that you would wish to change should you do the project again. Fill in your self evaluation sheet, and put together the end statements for the project.

# Space To Let   Planning for a parents' evening

In this project you are to organise and plan the next parents' evening for your class at your school.

You have to present your ideas firstly to your teacher or head teacher to get their approval. Secondly you have to produce the final presentation to tell them and the parents about the evening.

GET PERMISSION FOR YOUR PROJECT. DISCUSS IT WITH THE PEOPLE CONCERNED.

COLLECT INFORMATION ABOUT THE 'SPACE', AND THE 'EVENT'.

PRODUCE A PLAN VIEW DRAWING OF THE SPACE.

COMPARE YOUR DRAWING WITH THE REAL THING. ARE THERE THINGS TO ADD?

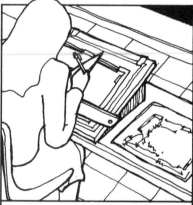

DRAW OUT YOUR PLAN NEATLY. TAKE CARE TO USE THE CORRECT SYMBOLS.

MAKE A LIST OF WHAT YOU NEED TO DO IN THE SPACE.

THINK ABOUT WHAT THIS MEANS IN TERMS OF THE FURNITURE AND FITTINGS.

PLAN OUT HOW YOU WANT TO ARRANGE THE ROOM. TRY OUT SEVERAL IDEAS.

# Space To Let   Planning for a parents' evening

DISCUSS YOUR IDEAS. MAKE NOTES OF ANY COMMENTS OR CHANGES.

MAKE A 'BRIEF' FOR THE PRESENTATION, SAYING WHAT IT HAS TO DO.

THINK ABOUT POSSIBLE IDEAS. SHOULD IT BE A POSTER ?

OR WOULD A 'LEAFLET' FOR PUPILS TO TAKE HOME BE BETTER ?

DO YOU NEED A REPORT TO SHOW YOUR DECISION MAKING ?

FINALLY, DRAW UP AND PRESENT YOUR WORK. DISCUSS ANY COMMENTS.

FILL IN YOUR EVALUATION SHEETS AND THEN THE 'END STATEMENTS'!

You will, no doubt, have been thinking about your presentation as you were doing it, and have come to some decisions about how good it was. Produce a questionnaire to check the opinions of the parents and others at the meeting.

Put up an exhibition of the work you have done for the project. Store your work carefully. Make records and take photographs of models, etc. in case they don't last.

## References

# Operator Interface    General idea

This project is about designing something that has to be operated by somebody else. It may be the actual workplace or the controls of a particular machine.

**Operator interface** is a technological way of saying the point where the machine and the person meet. The project is therefore concerned with the display of information and design of controls, and also the way things are arranged so that they best fit the user.

First you must find a situation that you can get access to, and which you feel could be improved. Find out what the user does. Record the things they do and their opinion of what they are doing. Your task is then to re-design their situation and present and test your ideas.

TALK TO THE PERSON AND FIND OUT THEIR OPINION OF THEIR WORK.

MAKE NOTES AND OBSERVATIONS OF THEM AT WORK.

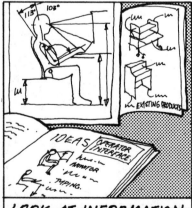

LOOK AT INFORMATION AND DATA ON ERGONOMICS AND ANTHROPOMETRICS.

THINK OF IDEAS FOR IMPROVEMENT. MODEL AND PRESENT YOUR IDEAS.

SET UP AND DISCUSS THE IDEAS WITH THE PERSON AT WORK. NOTE ANY COMMENTS.

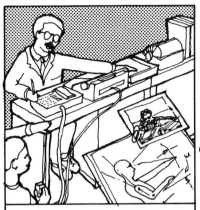

TAKE DETAILED MEASURE-
MENTS OF THE PERSON
AND THEIR WORKPLACE.

LOOK CAREFULLY AT THEM
WORKING. USE PHOTOS
AND VIDEO IF AVAILABLE.

INTERVIEW THE 'OPERATOR'
ABOUT HOW THEY FEEL. ASK
ABOUT ANY DISCOMFORT.

TRACE ANY ERGONOMIC
AND ANTHROPOMETRIC
DATA.

PRODUCE A DESIGN REPORT
LOOKING AT THE EXISTING
SITUATION.

USE MODELS AND PLANS.
SEE IF YOU CAN MAKE ANY
IMPROVEMENTS.

DISCUSS YOUR IDEAS WITH
THE OPERATOR. MAKE A
NOTE OF THEIR COMMENTS.

MAKE A MODEL SHOWING
YOUR IDEAS.

IF POSSIBLE, MOCK UP THE
IDEAS IN 'REAL LIFE' AND
RECORD THE RESULTS.

# Operator Interface   Washing machine control panel

The operator interface in this example is the control panel on an automatic washing machine. The areas you are concerned with are:

- the controls;
- display of information.

## Brief

Re-design the control panel of an automatic washing machine paying particular attention to the way it is used and the information that it needs to give the user.

You may assume that the controls can be changed in any way you wish providing they stay within the area of the existing front panel (size 300 × 100 mm).

MAKE DETAILED NOTES OF WHAT THE EXISTING PRODUCTS LOOK LIKE.

TALK TO SOMEONE WHO USES A WASHING MACHINE. RECORD THEIR COMMENTS.

CHECK ANY OTHER PRODUCT INFORMATION. MAKE NOTES ABOUT THE PRODUCTS.

First, you must find out what the existing controls are and what they do. Then use what you know about display graphics, ergonomics and controls to improve the layout and design.

Record the sequence of operations for using the machine. Are there things that the machine does that you have to tell the user about? Does the user need to know about fibres, fabrics, temperatures and wash cycles?

Put the operating instructions on to cards and construct a block diagram of the operations.

Collect information on as many kinds of switches and controls that you can. Choose ones that you think may be useful in this instance. Collect and record any general ergonomic information about the controls and displays. Record any particular bits that you think will be useful.

Are there particular things about the conditions that the switches and controls have to work in that makes certain types more suitable?

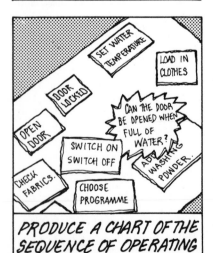

PRODUCE A CHART OF THE SEQUENCE OF OPERATING THE WASHING MACHINE.

THINK ABOUT POSSIBLE CONTROLS AND POSSIBLE ARRANGEMENTS.

# Operator Interface   Washing machine control panel

Design several alternative solutions as full-sized diagrams. You and your team can now discuss and decide which of the possibles to choose, or which bits from each are best.

DRAW OUT A SERIES OF POSSIBLE IDEAS.

DISCUSS THESE IDEAS AND CHOOSE THE ONE THAT IS EASIEST TO OPERATE.

MAKE A MODEL OF YOUR CHOSEN IDEA.

CHOOSE AND PRODUCE ANY INSTRUCTIONS OR GRAPHICS.

ASK SOMEONE TO FOLLOW THE OPERATING SEQUENCE.

LOOK CAREFULLY AT WHAT YOU HAVE PRODUCED. MAKE COMMENTS ON IT.

PRESENT YOUR DECISIONS AND YOUR FINAL IDEA. DISCUSS ANY COMMENTS.

### References

# Packaging Design   General idea

The idea of this project is to describe an object using drawings, then to use those drawings as a basis for designing and making a package to protect the object. Think carefully what the package has to do.

- It must protect the thing inside in many different situations – in the factory, in transit, in the shop, at home.
- It may carry information about the thing inside it, or give instructions about its safe and legal use.
- It may also give an impression or image of the product inside it.
- It should be made from flat material, paper or card.

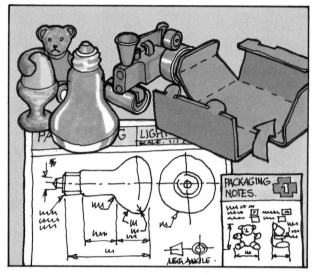

MEASURE AND SKETCH THE OBJECT THAT YOU ARE GOING TO PACKAGE.

PRODUCE AN ORTHOGRAPHIC DRAWING OF THE OBJECT.

MAKE A STUDY OF ALL TYPES OF EXISTING PACKAGING.

THINK UP A SERIES OF IDEAS FOR PACKAGING THE OBJECT.

MAKE UP PROTOTYPES FOR YOUR PACKAGE IDEAS. TEST THEM OUT.

CHOOSE THE BEST IDEA AND MAKE IT UP. DESIGN AND ADD GRAPHICS TO IT.

# Packaging Design A package for a light bulb

First measure and describe the light bulb with words, pictures and drawings. You may then decide to write down what the package should do or you may choose to produce your first idea and then test and judge it.

Collect old packaging. Flatten it out carefully, and draw the shape of the package. On the same piece of paper, make notes about the way it is held together, how strong it is, the kind of information that's on it, etc.

Often people have spent a long time designing and making the packages so that they work well. It is worth learning as much as you can from them. Look particularly at the way the tabs and folded parts are constructed.

When you have designed and made a package, you then have to say how well it works and how it could be improved. The true test would be to subject it to the same conditions it would meet in real life. You may choose to simulate this or just to give your opinion, rather than destroy your carefully made work. Say how you would improve the package if you were to re-design it.

The design of the graphics that go on to the package is, in itself, another design project (see Packaging and product graphics, page 91).

CHOOSE THE LIGHT BULB THAT YOU WISH TO MAKE A PACKAGE FOR.

TAKE MEASUREMENTS OF IT. MAKE A MODEL. NOTE ANY SPECIAL DETAILS.

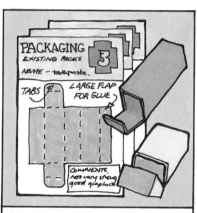

LOOK CAREFULLY AT HOW EXISTING PACKAGES ARE MADE.

THINK UP A SERIES OF POSSIBLE PACKAGES. MAKE UP AND TEST THEM.

CHOOSE YOUR BEST IDEA. DESIGN AND ADD SUITABLE GRAPHICS TO IT.

## References

# Pop-up Page

The idea of this project is to study the techniques that designers of pop-up books and cards use, in order to make your own pop-up page which will teach a child something.

Study as much pop-up material as you can and decide **what** you want your page to teach and **who** it is for.

DECIDE WHAT YOUR 'POP-UP' PAGE HAS TO SHOW, AND WHO IT IS AIMED AT.

LOOK AT EXISTING BOOKS AND MAKE NOTES ON THE WAY THINGS ARE DONE.

PUT TOGETHER A SERIES OF IDEAS THAT YOU MIGHT USE. TRY THEM OUT.

THEY WILL PROBABLY NEED SEVERAL ATTEMPTS BEFORE THEY WORK.

PLAN, CONSTRUCT, DRAW UP AND ILLUSTRATE YOUR 'POP-UP' PAGE.

TRY IT OUT ON THE CLIENT RECORD ANY COMMENTS, OR IMPROVEMENTS.

# Pop-up Page

You may need to study the way young children learn by watching them at play, by talking to parents and teachers, or by reading books about toy design.

Study existing pop-up books and cards and make models of particular mechanisms that interest you, making notes of any ideas that come to you for your own pop-up page.

THINK CAREFULLY ABOUT WHAT YOU ARE TRYING TO DO.

LOOK AT A SELECTION OF EXISTING BOOKS AND TECHNIQUES.

LOOK AT THE VARIOUS TECHNIQUES TO SEE WHICH THINGS WILL WORK BEST.

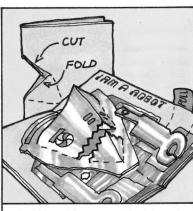

MAKE MODELS OF SOME IDEAS. EITHER COPY THEM OR INVENT YOUR OWN.

DECIDE THE THINGS YOU WANT TO TEACH, THEN DESIGN THE 'POP-UP' DETAILS.

Make sure that whatever you do is as carefully and neatly presented as possible. This will save disappointment and time. (Don't spoil a good idea with scruffy work.)

## References

PROJECT 10

In this project you have to research, build and test a model play structure for a children's playground. Firstly find a real place that you feel might need some kind of play structure. Find out (or imagine) who might use it, what age they are, what they want and what kind of games they want to play on it.

Look at structures around you, and see if there are any basic principles that you can establish. Collect together all of your information and put together as many ideas as you can. Test your ideas as models, discussing them with other people at all stages.

FIND OUT WHO MIGHT USE THE PLAY STRUCTURE.

WHAT ARE THE RULES AND PRINCIPLES ABOUT BUILDING A STRUCTURE?

WHAT MIGHT THE USERS WANT TO DO WITH IT?

MAKE A RECORD OF THE 'REQUIREMENTS' OF YOUR PLAY STRUCTURE.

DESIGN, BUILD AND TEST A MODEL OF YOUR IDEA FOR A STRUCTURE.

DISCUSS THIS WITH THE 'CLIENT'. MAKE NOTES ABOUT ANY CHANGES.

# Play Structure    General idea

It is always difficult to imagine what will happen to a structure when it is loaded unless you use models. Test-models made with plasticine or taped joints will exaggerate the effects of loading your structure, but will give you an excellent idea where the weak spots might be.

Always make the models as carefully as you can and, if you have tested them, always record what happened.

MAKE A QUICK MODEL TO TEST YOUR FIRST IDEAS ABOUT A STRUCTURE.

LOAD UP THE MODEL TO SEE WHERE THE WEAK POINTS ARE.

MAKE UP YOUR FINAL DESIGN AS A SCALE MODEL.

DISPLAY YOUR PROJECT WORK, DESCRIBE YOUR DESIGN, ANSWER QUERIES.

DISCUSS YOUR IDEAS AND PRESENTATION WITH THE 'CLIENT'!

Don't give up if your design doesn't work. Testing and improving your ideas is a valuable skill, which you should develop. It's better that you get your design 'right' now, rather than the structure be built and be a danger to the people using it.

# Play Structure   Primary school playground structure

This is an example of a real place that needs a play structure. A local primary school has a disused building in the playground. They wish to turn this building and the area in front of it into a play structure and a play area. Your task is to design and build a model of the area and a suitable play structure.

The pupils have been interviewed and the things that they want are:
- somewhere to play that they can imagine is a variety of things, like a fort or a shelter;
- somewhere that they can climb and run about.

The teachers would like the structure to be safe and easy to supervise. Parents would like it to be clean and safe, also easy to build as they have offered to build it!

Present and display your work well, take photographs of the models, or store them away carefully (perhaps make a special box to keep the models in). Write down any special comments that you have on the project, the way you worked and what you have produced.

Fill in your self assessment sheet, plus a record of the things that you have done as end statements.

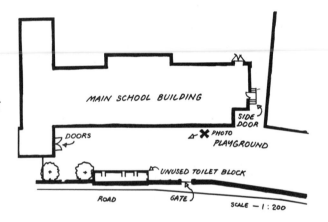

MAIN SCHOOL BUILDING

SIDE DOOR

DOORS         PHOTO
              PLAYGROUND

UNUSED TOILET BLOCK

ROAD      GATE

SCALE — 1 : 200

THESE ARE THE KIND OF MATERIALS THAT COULD BE USED.

PLAY STRUCTURES ARE NORMALLY BOLTED TOGETHER LIKE THIS.

TYRES AND ROPES ARE FIXED TOGETHER LIKE THIS.

FROM THE PLAN, MAKE A SCALE MODEL OF THE SPACE.

USE PLASTICINE AND STRAWS FOR TESTING OUT FIRST IDEAS.

TRY LOADING UP YOUR FIRST IDEAS STRUCTURE. NOTE WHAT HAPPENS.

MAKE NOTES AND DECIDE WHICH IS THE 'BEST' IDEA.

MAKE A CAREFUL MODEL OF YOUR CHOSEN IDEA.

PRODUCE ISOMETRIC AND ORTHOGRAPHIC DRAWINGS OF YOUR MODEL.

MAKE A DISPLAY TO PRESENT YOUR DRAWINGS AND MODEL.

ON YOUR EVALUATION SHEETS, RECORD WHAT YOU HAVE LEARNT.

## References

# Board Game Design

**PROJECT 12**

In this project you have to design a board game. The idea of the game is that you can win it only by cooperating with the other players rather than by competing against them. The end of the game and the point when everyone wins is when the last person finishes.

Write down as many games as you can, such as ludo and snakes and ladders, and make notes on:

- what the rules are;
- what things you have to be good at to win the game or what you have to do;
- what sort of people the game appeals to.

Are there basic kinds of games like escape games, memory games or strategy games?

See if you can change the rules or the theme of the game to make it cooperative. Discuss and write down your ideas.

**LOOK AT EXISTING BOARD GAMES AND WORK OUT THE NEW RULES.**

**SEE IF YOU CAN COME UP WITH IDEAS FOR YOUR OWN GAME.**

**TRY OUT YOUR IDEAS BEFORE YOU CHOOSE THE BEST ONE.**

**TRY PLAYING YOUR GAME. DISCUSS IT WITH OTHER PEOPLE.**

**FINALLY DESIGN, DRAW, COLOUR IN AND TEST YOUR NEW GAME.**

# Board Game Design

What might you do to make a game cooperative?

- Give advantages for cooperative play, and disadvantages for not.
- Make it possible to share ideas and information.
- Allow negotiation between players as to what to do and why.

With changed rules and a little imagination, design your own game. Try changing the theme or putting it into the past or the future. Experiment with possible layouts and alternative rules. Discuss your ideas as you go along.

Produce a trial version and see if you can play it. Incorporate any changes that come out as a result of trying out the game.

Finally, draw it out carefully, colour it in and make the pieces.

TAKE AN EXISTING BOARD GAME AND WRITE OUT THE RULES.

LOOK AT THE BASIC IDEAS USED IN GAMES (ESCAPE GAMES, OBSTACLES).

DISCUSS THE NEW GAME AND THE POSSIBILITIES.

WRITE OUT THE RULES FOR THE NEW GAME.

DEVISE, PLAN THE LAYOUT AND THE PIECES FOR THE NEW GAME.

DRAW, COLOUR IN AND TEST YOUR NEW GAME DESIGN.

## References

## PROJECT 13

# Non Comprendo   Non-written explanations

Imagine that you find yourself in a situation where you speak very little of the language, and you have to tell someone how to do something. That is exactly the situation in this project.

You have to explain how to do something using as few words as possible. The example I have given of making bread gave me quite a few problems and you can probably think of better ways of showing some of the stages.

The basic steps are:

- Talk to an expert about the thing that you are trying to describe.
- Decide what the stages of the process are.
- Find the best way of showing each stage graphically.
- Test how well you have done by asking someone to try and follow your instructions.

WATCH THE PROCESS CAREFULLY. TALK TO THE PERSON DOING IT.

MAKE CAREFUL RECORDS OF THE PROCESS.

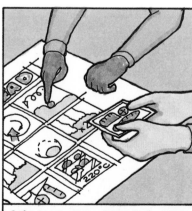

CHANGE THE PROCESS INTO A SERIES OF PICTURES. USE AS FEW WORDS AS POSSIBLE.

# Non Comprendo Techniques

TRY TO SIMPLIFY THE PICTURES SO THAT THEY ARE EASY TO UNDERSTAND.

CHOOSE THE KIND OF DRAWING CAREFULLY, TO AVOID CONFUSION.

ENLARGE AREAS, SO THAT CERTAIN THINGS CAN BE SHOWN MORE CLEARLY.

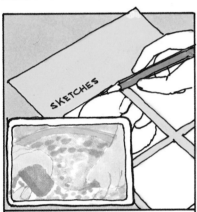

USE PHOTOGRAPHS AS VISUAL REFERENCES FOR YOUR DRAWINGS.

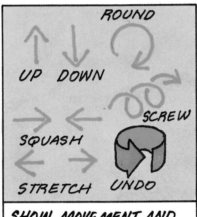

SHOW MOVEMENT AND DIRECTIONS WITH CARE. ALWAYS AVOID CONFUSION.

Presenting actions and objects can be quite difficult. Use whatever help you can, for example, photographs or video recordings. Any way of stopping the action and making it easier to draw things is worth trying.

You will also need to come to some decision about the viewpoint of the sequence. Do you draw as though you were watching it being done or as you would see it if you were doing it? (Both have been used in this book – which do you think works best?)

AVOID DAMAGING ERRORS. PRODUCE YOUR WORK IN PIECES, THEN PASTE IT UP.

GET SOMEONE TO TRY OUT YOUR WORK BY WORKING TO YOUR INSTRUCTIONS.

SKETCH FIRST, THEN LINE IN, AND FINALLY TRACE YOUR DRAWINGS.

# Non Comprendo  Wiring a plug

This is an actual example that you can try. You have to describe how to wire a three pin plug. First you have to draw the plug and all its parts as engineering drawings. Secondly work out the sequence of putting it together. This will not only make you aware of the parts of the object but will also give you an idea of how to wire it up.

**Make sure that the plug is not connected to anything.**

Take the plug apart **very carefully.**

Make a careful note of the stages of the operation. Be particularly careful of any difficult or fiddley bits which are hard to undo.

Carefully measure the pieces and do the detail drawings for each piece.

Put the plug back together from your notes (in the reverse order). Don't forget to include how to prepare the wires for connection. The colours of the wires are **extremely important**.

Remember the sequence of:
1. Planning.
2. Doing sketch drawings.
3. Improving and changing these drawings.
4. Producing final drawings.

Don't expect to be able to do final drawings without preparation and planning. If you look at pages 72–5 you will see that professional designers use a similar process to the one above.

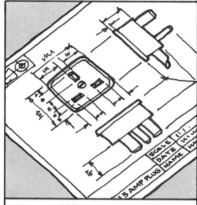

PRODUCE A DRAWING OF THE PLUG ASSEMBLY.

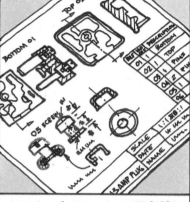

TAKE IT APART, MEASURE, SKETCH AND DRAW THE INDIVIDUAL PIECES.

RECORD THE SEQUENCE OF WIRING A PLUG PLUS IDEAS FOR DRAWING IT.

The way you decide to present your sequence will depend on **who** you are doing it for and **what use** they will make of it. A poster for the classroom wall and a flip-chart can tell the same story but in different ways. Try out different ways of presenting the information, until you get one that you think works well.

DISCUSS POSSIBLE WAYS OF SHOWING THE SEQUENCE.

SKETCH THE SEQUENCE AND THE KIND OF DRAWINGS THAT YOU WILL NEED.

# Non Comprendo  Wiring a plug

SKETCH, TRACE AND LINE IN THE FINAL DRAWINGS OF THE PROCESS.

PASTE UP THE DRAWINGS IN THE CORRECT SEQUENCE.

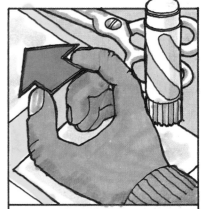

ADD ANY EXTRA DETAILS.

PUT ANY LETTERING ON TO YOUR DRAWINGS.

GET SOMEONE TO WIRE THE PLUG FOLLOWING YOUR INSTRUCTIONS.

Test your work by asking someone to follow your instructions and watch carefully what they do. Write down any questions that they ask, and record their comments and suggestions. Correct and modify your work as a result of this test and then draw out the final version.

Make sure you enter what you have done and how well you did it on your self evaluation sheet/ end statements/course chart.

## References

**Safety note**
**If you are in any doubt over electrical equipment seek advice. Don't risk your life.**

# Local Issue    General idea

Wherever you live there will be changes which affect the lives of the people around you. These are **local issues**. The size or nature of the changes are not important for this project.

What you have to do is to take a local issue and present the case for and against the changes graphically.

- Decide **who** the information is for.
- Decide **what** they need to know.

It is then up to you to design the best way of communicating the information to them.

*MAKE RECORDS OF THE SITUATION AS IT IS NOW.*

It is quite difficult when you start a project like this to decide what information you need and where to get it from. These are some ideas that might help.

- Try and talk to an 'expert' and ask their advice.
- Use brainstorming (see page 37) to see what kinds of local issues there might be.
- Talk to your local librarian. They are usually very skilled in helping people to find information.

*INTERVIEW PEOPLE AND GET THEIR OPINIONS ON THE PROPOSED CHANGES.*

*ANALYSE THE RESULTS OF YOUR QUESTIONNAIRE.*

*TURN THE RESULTS INTO GRAPHS AND CHARTS.*

*DRAW OUT, OR TURN INTO A DISPLAY, THE PROPOSED CHANGES.*

Start with finding out what the situation is now and think about the best way of presenting this. What is the situation going to be in the future? What are the predicted effects of the future situation on the people concerned?

Conduct a survey of opinions based on your descriptions of the present and future situation and then chart the results of your survey.

Possible information sources:
- Newspapers
- Photographs
- Magazines
- Local radio
- Reports and reference books
- Local history books
- Libraries

DISCUSS YOUR IDEAS ON THE 'LOCAL ISSUE'. WHAT MORE DO YOU NEED TO KNOW?

When you have decided which issue to choose, you may need to explore certain facts or viewpoints in greater depth, so that you feel that you have the whole story. Your presentation should aim to show an unbiased view. (Giving the same treatment to both sides of the argument.)

DECIDE ON THE BEST WAY TO FIND THINGS OUT.

ALWAYS TEST YOUR IDEAS BEFORE YOU START TO COLLECT INFORMATION.

When you have put your story together you have then to decide the 'best' way of presenting it to the people concerned. Look at what public information methods exist at the moment, but also try to think of something that will be eye catching or entertaining and will get your ideas across most effectively.

DECIDE HOW TO PRESENT YOUR SURVEY AND THE RESULTS.

ASK FOR COMMENTS ON THE 'LOCAL ISSUE' AND YOUR PRESENTATION OF IT.

# Local Issue   Nuclear power

Nuclear power is a possible local issue you could use. You may actually have a nuclear reactor in your neighbourhood; or perhaps the storage and disposal of nuclear waste is an issue. If not, you could imagine that a proposal has been made to build a reactor or to store waste in your area.

Gather as much information and as many opinions as you can. Then what you must try to do is to present **both** sides of the case as fairly as possible.

The information you will need to collect might include:

The types of power station in Britain (see the table below): Which generates the most electricity? Which is the most efficient? Which produces the cheapest electricity?

The types of nuclear reactor: Which is the cheapest to build? Which has the longest life? Which is the safest?

The risk of leakages and melt-downs such as at Chernobyl: What is the likelihood of more accidents like this? How soon could people be evacuated?

Nuclear waste: How safely can it be stored/disposed of?

Sizewell A nuclear power station in Suffolk

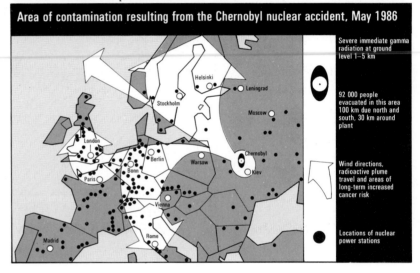

**Area of contamination resulting from the Chernobyl nuclear accident, May 1986**

Severe immediate gamma radiation at ground level 1–5 km

92 000 people evacuated in this area 100 km due north and south, 30 km around plant

Wind directions, radioactive plume travel and areas of long-term increased cancer risk

Locations of nuclear power stations

**Location of power stations at 31 March 1987**

| | Declared net capability megawatts sent out | No. of stations |
|---|---|---|
| Coal-fired | 30 537 | 37 |
| Coal/gas-fired | 366 | 1 |
| Coal/oil-fired | 4 504 | 3 |
| Oil-fired | 6 775 | 7 |
| Nuclear | 5 029 | 10 |
| Gas-turbine | 1 442 | 11 |
| Hydro | 112 | 7 |
| Pumped-storage | 2 088 | 2 |
| Auxiliary gas-turbines | 1 510 | — |
| Total | 52 363 | 78 |

# Local Issue  Nuclear power

Collect your own information about this topic. Check to see whether you have been given an unbiased view of the situation. Start to think about how you are going to get the opinion of people around you on this topic.

It can be quite difficult to produce a questionnaire that works.

1. Be very clear what you want to know.
2. Take care that you are not influencing people's answers by the way you ask the questions.

CHECK THE INFORMATION PROVIDED AGAINST YOUR OWN RESEARCH.

FIND OUT WHAT THE PLANS AND PREDICTIONS FOR THE FUTURE ARE.

CAREFULLY PUT TOGETHER YOUR QUESTIONNAIRE.

TRY OUT YOUR QUESTIONS ON A SMALL GROUP, THEN ON A LARGER SAMPLE.

Try out your questions on someone before you begin your 'proper' survey.

Interviewing people can take a long time. You may decide to write the questionnaire jointly in a group and then share the load of asking the questions.

ANALYSE THE RESULTS. PUT THEM INTO GRAPHICAL FORM.

MAKE A DISPLAY OF YOUR WORK ON THIS PROJECT. ASK FOR COMMENTS.

## References

# Systems Design  Basic principles

Much of the skill in designing things comes from thinking about them in a way that allows you to come up with your own ideas. Try to think about them in questions rather than answers. One of the simplest ways of doing this is to try to think about 'what things do' in general rather than specific terms.

In this project you are asked to take a well-known object and break it down into its basic and general functions. Then explore the possibilities of different ways of achieving the same functions, and the possibilities for designing a **new** object.

Most designers arrive at a way of working which uses a certain amount of 'system', but only as much as is useful. At first you may find this approach difficult but it is important that you develop the technique of being able to deal with complicated design situations and this is one way of doing so.

Simple questions like **who?, how?, what?, where?, when?, why?,** can be very helpful.

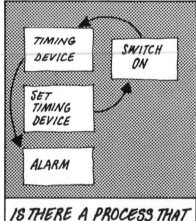

**TRY TO THINK OF ALL THE THINGS THAT YOU NEED TO KNOW. PUT THEM IN ORDER.**

**IS THERE A PROCESS THAT HAS TO BE FOLLOWED?**

**CAN YOU ANSWER THE QUESTIONS WHO, WHAT, WHY, WHERE?**

**IS THERE A WAY OF SHOWING THE ALTERNATIVE SOLUTIONS?**

# Systems Design    Basic principles

**BRAINSTORMING. PUT AS MANY IDEAS DOWN AS YOU CAN. THEN CLASSIFY THEM.**

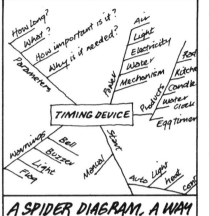

**A SPIDER DIAGRAM. A WAY OF TRYING TO RELATE TOPICS, IDEAS AND INFORMATION.**

Brainstorming is a technique of listing all the ideas that you can think of and then attempting to sort them into some kind of order.

1.  Write down all the things that you can think of. (No matter how silly they might be!)
2.  Put these ideas into broad categories.
3.  Are there any areas that you can see that you have forgotten or are there any good ideas for answering the problem?

The spider diagram is a similar way of deciding 'what you need to know' by using branches along which you write the general headings which divide as required.

There are often ways of showing a process simply as a chart, and then using the chart as a way to look at the needs of a design. The way that systems design works is to try to say things in a general way first, and then to become more specific as time goes on. Systems can often be shown best as a report, or a chart.

Systems can only help you to get answers, you still have to think of the ideas yourself. Remember no one else works in quite the same way as you, so you must try and get a system that works for you.

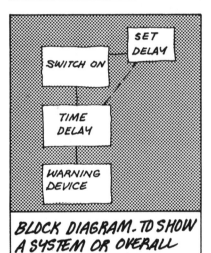

**BLOCK DIAGRAM. TO SHOW A SYSTEM OR OVERALL IDEA FOR A MACHINE.**

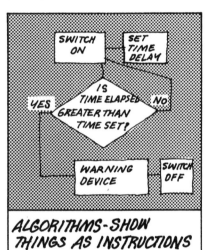

**ALGORITHMS - SHOW THINGS AS INSTRUCTIONS OR YES/NO DECISIONS.**

**CHARTS CAN RELATE IDEAS TO ACTUAL OBJECTS AS POSSIBLE ANSWERS.**

## CONTENTS

**DESIGN REPORTS - SET OUT RESEARCH, IDEAS, EXISTING PRODUCTS AND DISCUSSIONS.**

# Systems Design    Automatic animal feeder

In this project you have to imagine that you are the person whose job it is to provide all the information so that someone else can do the designing.

*WHAT POSSIBILITIES ARE THERE? HOW CAN SYSTEMS HELP?*

A group of pupils, younger than you, have the task of designing and making an automatic animal feeder. It is your job to provide them with as much information as they need to do this.

If you were doing the designing yourself there would probably be short cuts that could save you time. But since you are doing this for someone who's not as good a designer as you, it is important that you don't miss anything out or make things too complicated.

Remember the idea is not for you to give them the answer, but for you to provide a range of ideas and information from which they can arrive at their **own** solution.

*WRITE DOWN ALL OF THE THINGS YOU CAN THINK OF. PUT SIMILAR THINGS TOGETHER.*

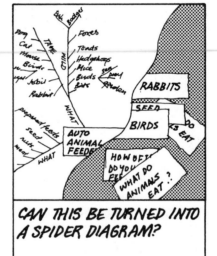

*CAN THIS BE TURNED INTO A SPIDER DIAGRAM?*

The chart on the left shows the main steps of a feeder. You have to provide the answers to **what?, how?, who?, why?, where?, when?** for each step. It may be worth thinking at this point of what the best way to present this information would be.

Whilst you are collecting and presenting the information for the system you will probably have ideas as to how to solve this particular design problem. Make a note of these ideas for use later on.

STORE FOOD

FILL WITH FOOD

DISPLAY FOOD

DELIVER FOOD TO THE ANIMAL

*IS THERE A BLOCK DIAGRAM WHICH APPLIES TO YOUR ANIMAL FEEDER?*

# Systems Design   Automatic animal feeder

Look at and record details of products which you have seen that do the same job. Make descriptions of how they work. What are their good and bad points?

Are there any other ideas that might be useful, like ways of releasing small amounts of food, or ways of food being released by light or darkness?

You may need to draw out some parts of these ideas in detail so that the young designers can apply them to their own work. Try to make a chart of the ideas so that a number of 'concepts' can be chosen.

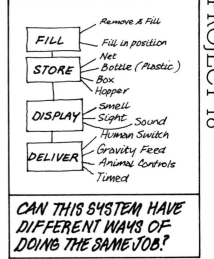

CAN THIS SYSTEM HAVE DIFFERENT WAYS OF DOING THE SAME JOB?

Think about the abilities of the people who are going to design and make the object. You may need to go and interview them, maybe take photographs of them at work.

WHAT ARE THE STUDENTS' ABILITIES? WHAT CAN THEY UNDERSTAND?

The difficult job is now to present all of the information and ideas that you have collected, in a way that the young designers can easily understand. Remember also that the more interesting it looks the more they are likely to read it.

**Teachers' note**   You may wish to split this project into two halves:
1. Writing the design specification for an automatic animal feeder.
2. Converting this information into material suitable for young designers.

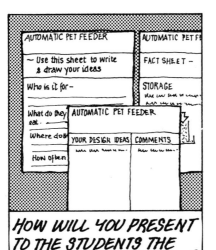

HOW WILL YOU PRESENT TO THE STUDENTS THE THINGS YOU HAVE DONE?

### References

# Teach Me!   General idea

Imagine that you are put in the position of having to explain in detail to someone how something is made and put together. A typical example would be a maintenance manual or assembly instructions. The difficulties are to decide which kind of drawings are of most use to people, and then to present the information in the correct and most suitable way.

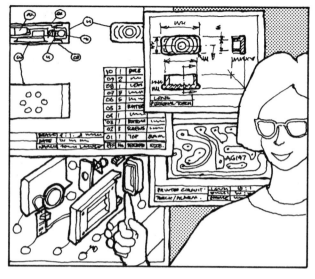

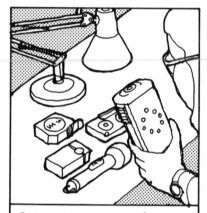

DECIDE ON THE OBJECT YOU ARE GOING TO USE. PICK SOMETHING SIMPLE.

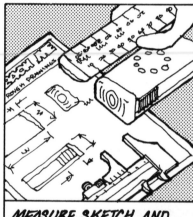

MEASURE, SKETCH AND MAKE DETAILED DRAWINGS OF IT.

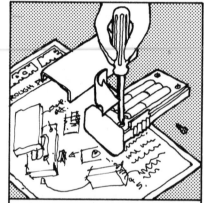

TAKE IT APART, RECORD THE SEQUENCE, SKETCH AND DRAW THE PIECES.

MEASURE CAREFULLY. ADD THE SIZES TO THE SKETCHES.

TALK ABOUT WHICH PEOPLE NEED INFORMATION AND WHAT IT IS THEY NEED.

PUT THE DETAILS ON TO A CHART.

## Teach Me!   General idea

You will need to think of the kind of presentation you need for each person's requirements. What do they know and how do they work at present? How is it best to give information? Engineering drawing is probably going to be the best method for most things, but there may be better ways of describing objects or processes.

**CHECK TO SEE YOU HAVE ALL THE INFORMATION THAT YOU NEED.**

**IS THERE AN OVERALL STYLE THAT YOU WANT YOUR WORK TO HAVE?**

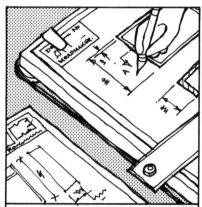

**DRAW THE DETAILED DRAWINGS OF THE PARTS OF THE OBJECT.**

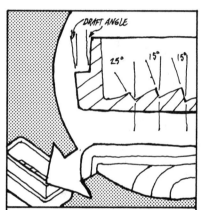

**PUT DIMENSIONS ON TO THESE DRAWINGS. HOW ARE THE PIECES MADE?**

**SOME PIECES MAY HAVE TO BE DRAWN AT DIFFERENT SCALES.**

**WILL YOU NEED A DRAWING SHOWING HOW THE PIECES FIT TOGETHER?**

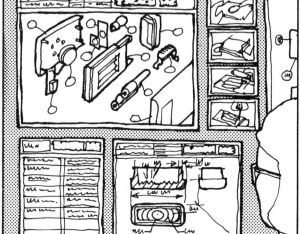

# Teach Me! Battery torch

This is an example of a torch. Get hold of a similar one or estimate the sizes from the photograph opposite.

- Work out the sizes of the pieces and produce sketch drawings of them.
- Work out and list how the pieces fit together.
- Discuss and work out the way the pieces are made and from what material.

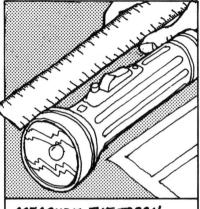

MEASURE THE TORCH, SKETCH THE OUTSIDE AND ADD THE DIMENSIONS.

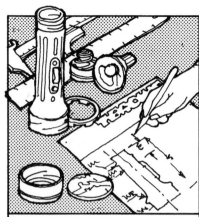

TAKE IT APART, RECORD THE SEQUENCE AND HOW THE PIECES FIT TOGETHER.

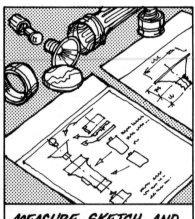

MEASURE, SKETCH AND DIMENSION THE PIECES.

It is very important that you measure the pieces accurately. You may need to seek some help in using tools like vernier calipers or micrometers.

Get someone to take the torch apart and record how they do it. Photographs and video recordings will be extremely helpful.

You need to decide what kinds of drawings are suitable for the people involved in making and assembling the torch.

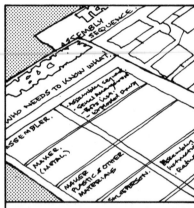

DECIDE WHO NEEDS WHICH KIND OF INFORMATION WHEN MAKING THE TORCH.

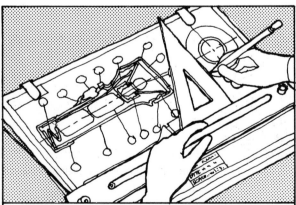

PRODUCE A CROSS SECTION DRAWING. SHOW WHAT ALL THE PIECES ARE CALLED AND HOW THEY FIT TOGETHER.

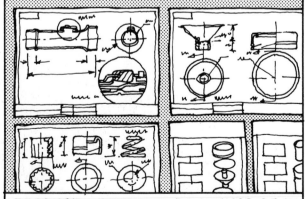

PRODUCE DETAILED DRAWINGS OF ALL OF THE PIECES PLUS DIMENSIONS.

# Teach Me! Battery torch

Whilst there may seem to be lots of complicated rules about engineering drawings, remember that the main aim is to provide the information in a way that can be understood by a wide range of people. It should be possible to follow the instructions on the drawings easily and without the object being wrongly made. If you feel that some parts of the assembly are better understood as pictorial drawings, then draw them that way, but be careful.

**ASK SOMEONE ELSE TO TAKE THE TORCH APART AND WATCH WHAT THEY DO.**

**MAKE A CHART TO SHOW THE ASSEMBLY SEQUENCE.**

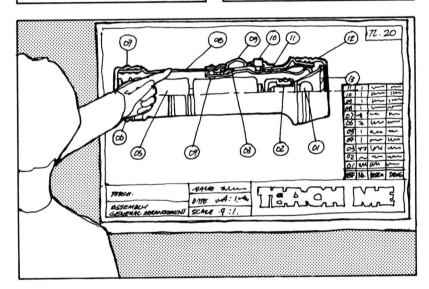

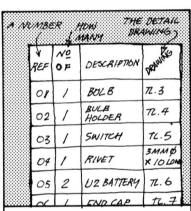

| REF | NO OF | DESCRIPTION | DRAWING |
|-----|-------|-------------|---------|
| 01 | 1 | BULB | TL.3 |
| 02 | 1 | BULB HOLDER | TL.4 |
| 03 | 1 | SWITCH | TL.5 |
| 04 | 1 | RIVET | 3MM Ø X 10 LONG |
| 05 | 2 | U2 BATTERY | TL.6 |
| 06 | 1 | END CAP | TL.7 |

**REMEMBER, PUT A PARTS LIST ON TO YOUR ASSEMBLY DRAWING.**

## References

- Engineering drawing 76–80
- Hidden detail 59
- Measurement 103
- Orthographic drawing 54–60
- Picturing techniques 48
- Scale 52
- Sectioning 59

Remember to fill in your self evaluation sheet/end statements /course chart.

# Skills Introduction

**How to use this section** The remainder of the book deals with particular skills. It is intended to be used as a reference section to satisfy the particular needs of the projects at the standard necessary for the examination. Students do not need to cover all of the skills sections. The sections are not in any particular order.

Fundamental to all of the skill areas are the processes of
- planning;
- decision making;
- layout in rough form;
- modification and correction;
- production of the final version.

Teachers and students are encouraged to devise their own tests and games in order to reinforce the students' grasp of these skills.

# Basics in Communication

Each piece of work you produce has a purpose. Ask yourself:

- Who is it for?
- Why do they need it?
- What do they need, or what do they have to do with it?
- Where is it going to be used?
- When is it going to be used?
- For how long is it useful?

Be aware that whilst you don't have to stick to them, there are stages of planning, designing, making and testing.

The most important of these is the testing, in that each part of each idea has to be thought about and tested (perhaps only in your head) to see if it will work. Ideas that don't work should be modified or rejected. Testing goes on throughout all the other stages.

It is always better to discuss your work with someone else, partly to get your own thoughts clear and partly to get their opinions. Very often you will find the answer to a problem by having to explain it to another person.

Designing is a very personal thing, it can start with vague ideas that slowly become clearer and more 'real', or it may be a series of complete ideas. What you must try to become aware of is how **you** design things and how **you** can improve what you do.

# Paste-up and Basic Equipment

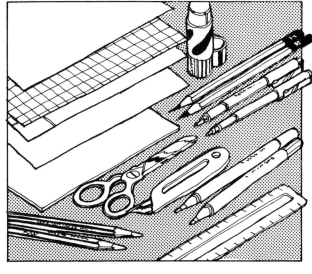

Throughout this book you are encouraged to present your work as well as you can. This is not just because it makes things nice to look at, or because you will be pleased with what you have done. The course is about **communication**. The better you present something, the easier it will be for others to understand it.

Try to develop the skill of thinking ahead and imagining where the difficulties might lie. Try things out in advance and avoid making stupid mistakes. The most frustrating mistake to make is to ruin hours of work in a careless few seconds. This often happens when you are tired or under pressure.

## Pencils

The hardness of the lead is shown by the letter at the end of the pencil:
H (hard), 2H, 3H... (harder)
HB – for general use
B (soft), 2B, 3B... (softer)
Pens and automatic pencils come with certain line widths, from 0.1 (very thin) to 1.0 (very thick). A normal selection you might use would be 0.35, 0.5 and 0.7.

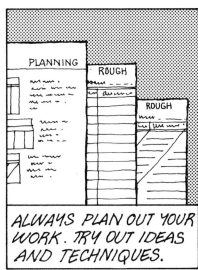

ALWAYS PLAN OUT YOUR WORK. TRY OUT IDEAS AND TECHNIQUES.

DRAW THINGS AS SEPARATE PIECES THEN STICK THEM IN PLACE.

CHOOSE LAYOUT AND GRAPHICS TO GIVE THE DESIRED 'EFFECT'.

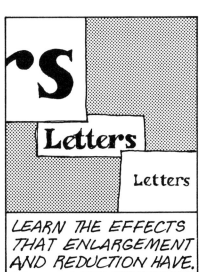

LEARN THE EFFECTS THAT ENLARGEMENT AND REDUCTION HAVE.

Plan out your work from sketches (called roughs but this doesn't mean that you mustn't be careful) through to the finished thing. Use a paste-up. Do the work in stages and stick the pieces together finally as a finished item. This book was done in exactly that way.

# Picturing Techniques

Picturing techniques are to do with representing three-dimensional objects in two dimensions. All the techniques are useful, though you may find some easier than others.

The fundamental idea is to look at an object and be able to see the object in your head. Following that, if you can imagine what the object will look like if you change the position that you are looking at it from, then you are most of the way there.

Whilst some people will have a better developed drawing ability, there are very few people who cannot learn to represent things using a few basic techniques. It may take time and practice but it **is** possible.

Your brain will always try to make sense of what it sees, and will try and fill in the gaps between a drawing and a real object. (For example, look at the side and plan views on the far right.)

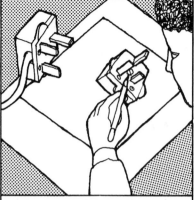

THERE IS NO SUBSTITUTE FOR 'LOOKING' AND DRAWING WHAT YOU SEE.

PERSPECTIVE DRAWING CAN HELP TO GIVE A REALISTIC IMAGE.

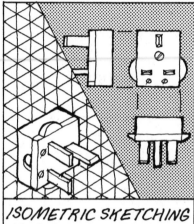

ISOMETRIC SKETCHING IS A QUICK WAY OF GETTING AN IMAGE.

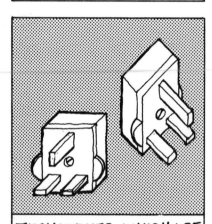

TECHNIQUES WHICH USE SIDE OR PLAN VIEWS CAN GIVE HELPFUL IMAGES.

TRY TO 'IMAGINE' THE OBJECT IN YOUR HEAD BEFORE YOU DRAW IT.

A WAY TO CHECK YOUR DRAWING IS TO LOOK AT IT FROM THE BACK.

## References

# Perspective Drawing

Of the picturing techniques used, perspective drawing tries to make things look most **real.** If you take a photograph of an object, you can trace the vanishing points, and see for yourself how the rules work about things getting smaller and closer together as they get further away from you.

Try to decide what kind of view of the object you want. Look at the effect that the viewpoint has on the position of the horizon and vanishing points. The number of vanishing points that you choose depends on the kind of view of the object that you want.

Use the techniques that you find easiest and that communicate the object best. For curved and complicated objects it is probably easier to imagine the object is inside a box, to plot the box, and then to draw the object inside it.

## References

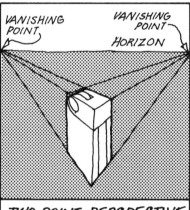

PERSPECTIVE DRAWING GIVES YOU THE MOST REALISTIC IMAGES.

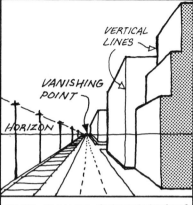

ONE POINT PERSPECTIVE. NOTICE THE VERTICAL AND HORIZONTAL LINES.

TWO POINT PERSPECTIVE. TWO 'VANISHING' POINTS.

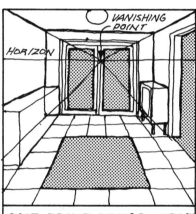

ONE POINT PERSPECTIVE IS PARTICULARLY GOOD FOR DRAWINGS OF ROOMS

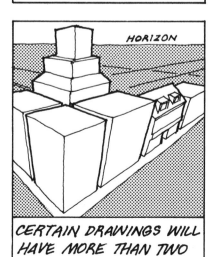

WIDENING THE V P'S WILL MAKE THE IMAGE MORE REALISTIC.

CERTAIN DRAWINGS WILL HAVE MORE THAN TWO VANISHING POINTS.

# Isometric Drawing

Isometric drawing is the simplest of the picturing techniques: the objects are drawn with lines that are either at 30 degrees to the horizon or vertical. It is normally assumed that the lengths of lines are the true lengths. This is not actually correct so things will always look slightly too big.

Isometric drawing is a good way of getting an accurate picture of how an object might look, quickly and simply. Grid paper with isometric lines on it can help when sketching ideas, as long as you try to see the object in your head and then see how it fits on to the grid paper.

Isometric circles are drawn using a true view of a circle and slicing it into sections then taking the lengths of the sections and drawing them at 30 degrees to the circle centre line.

Not all lines will be at 30 degrees but, as with perspective drawing, imagine the object is in a box, draw the box and then the object within it.

ISOMETRIC GRID PAPER GIVES A QUICK IDEA OF HOW AN OBJECT LOOKS.

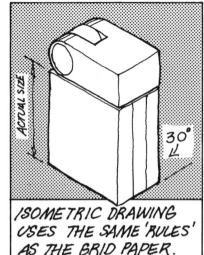

ISOMETRIC DRAWING USES THE SAME 'RULES' AS THE GRID PAPER.

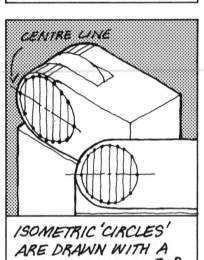

ISOMETRIC 'CIRCLES' ARE DRAWN WITH A CENTRE LINE AT 30°.

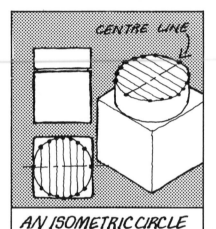

AN ISOMETRIC CIRCLE DRAWN IN THE HORIZONTAL PLANE.

TO DRAW LINES NOT AT 30° - PLOT THE END POINTS AND JOIN THE DOTS.

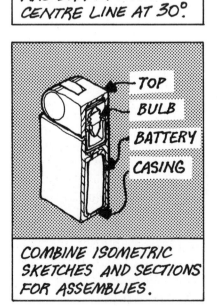

TOP
BULB
BATTERY
CASING

COMBINE ISOMETRIC SKETCHES AND SECTIONS FOR ASSEMBLIES.

## References

# Other Picturing Techniques

So that you can get an idea of how an object might look, a front or plan view is a good technique to start with. The view is then given a thickness. The kind of picture you get does not look much like the object in real life, but it can help you to see the object in your head.

This technique can be useful for buildings where you start with a plan of the ground floor (normally turned at 45 degrees) and then work upwards.

It can simplify exploded drawings, making them easier to draw yet still understandable. Choose the view carefully.

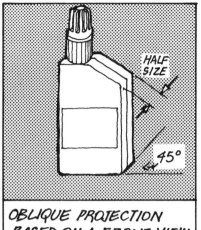

OBLIQUE PROJECTION BASED ON A FRONT VIEW ADDING 'THICKNESS' AT 45°.

AN EFFECTIVE METHOD FOR 'EXPLODED' VIEWS.

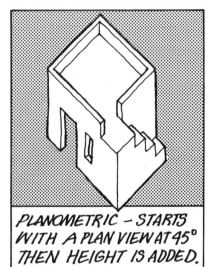

PLANOMETRIC – STARTS WITH A PLAN VIEW AT 45° THEN HEIGHT IS ADDED.

GOOD FOR DRAWINGS OF BUILDINGS AND ASSEMBLIES.

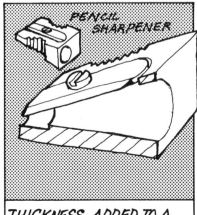

THICKNESS ADDED TO A SECTION CAN MAKE IT EASIER TO UNDERSTAND.

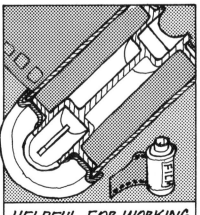

HELPFUL FOR WORKING OUT HOW PIECES FIT TOGETHER.

This technique can also be of use when you are designing pieces that fit together, where a section of the parts can be given depth to increase the reality and help you to imagine what the result will look like.

# Scale

The ability to enlarge or reduce a drawing relative
to the actual size of the object is important for
several reasons.

1. It means that you don't have to have a piece of
   paper as big as the object. Quite difficult if it is a
   room you are drawing!
2. You can improve the accuracy of your drawing,
   by drawing the object bigger than it actually is.

It is easy to see that when drawing a complex object
various scales may be necessary to explain all of the
details. (For example, what scale would you use for
showing the microchip circuitry and the case of a
radio?)

THE SCALE OF YOUR DRAWING WILL
NEED TO CHANGE — DEPENDING
ON WHAT YOU ARE TRYING TO SHOW.

THE DRAWING MAY NEED
TO BE LARGER THAN THE
ACTUAL OBJECT (2:1).

FOR BUILDING DRAWINGS
THE DRAWING WILL BE
SMALLER THAN THE OBJECT.

Scale is represented by:
- 1:10 means the drawing is
  one-tenth of the actual size
- 1:50 one-fiftieth of the actual
  size
- 2:1 drawn twice as big as
  actual size
- 1:2 half as big as actual size

Getting used to scale drawing can
be difficult at first, so here are two
tips:
- Write the scaled dimensions
  on to the drawing in coloured
  crayon.
- Make or buy a scale ruler, or
  draw a scaled ruler along the
  bottom of your page, and take
  your measurements from it.

## References

- All of the project work and
  most of the drawings that you
  do will involve using scales of
  various sorts.

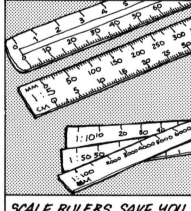

SCALE RULERS SAVE YOU
HAVING TO WORK OUT THE
'SCALED' SIZES.

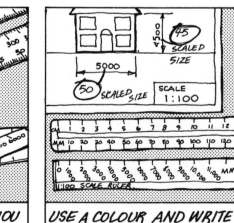

USE A COLOUR AND WRITE
IN THE 'SCALED' SIZES.

# Rotating Views

Drawing rotating views helps with the skill of imaging an object in your head and then imagining what you would see if you looked at it from a different position. Practise by drawing things as you see them, but also from angles different to the way you are looking at them (plan views/front views).

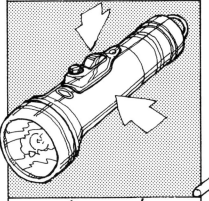

TRY TO 'IMAGINE' THAT YOU CAN SEE THE OBJECT IN YOUR HEAD.

TRY TO 'IMAGINE' WHAT THE FRONT AND PLAN VIEWS WILL LOOK LIKE.

WHAT IF YOU WANT TO LOOK CLOSELY AT THE SWITCH AREA?

Drawing an object exactly as you see it is quite difficult. Try using isometric or perspective grid paper to help you. Now take the same object and try to draw what it looks like from a different view.

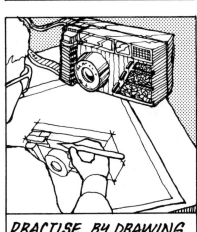

PRACTISE BY DRAWING AN OBJECT AS YOU SEE IT.

Work in pairs and test each other by one person holding the object and asking the other to draw a different view of the object. Practise close-up views of parts of the object seen from a different angle. This is a skill which you will be using throughout your design career. Think about it whenever you describe and design things.

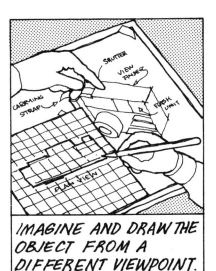

IMAGINE AND DRAW THE OBJECT FROM A DIFFERENT VIEWPOINT.

# Orthographics General

This technique was developed to simplify drawings that people making things needed in order to put them together. The drawings should **avoid** confusion, although initially, it can be quite difficult to understand what is happening and what the views mean.

What you are trying to do is to look at an object from **directly** in front, to the side, or on top of it (ignoring things like perspective). Different people will have different ways of understanding orthographic drawings. Always try to see the object in your head, and fit in the details from the orthographic views.

AN ORTHOGRAPHIC DRAWING SHOWS DIFFERENT VIEWS OF THE OBJECT - NORMALLY FRONT, SIDE AND PLAN.

FIRST ANGLE PROJECTION. PROJECT WHAT YOU SEE PAST THE OBJECT.

THIRD ANGLE PROJECTION- PROJECT WHAT YOU SEE IN FRONT OF THE OBJECT.

FIRST ANGLE PROJECTION. LIKE SLIDING THE OBJECT AROUND A SPHERE.

FIRST ANGLE PROJECTION LOOKS LIKE THIS. SYMBOL

THIRD ANGLE PROJECTION LOOKS LIKE THIS. SYMBOL

People often talk about being able to **read** an orthographic drawing. It is a visual language for describing objects and processes.

In this book, first angle projection is used throughout (apart from the section on third angle projection). This is only to avoid confusion, not because one method is any easier than the other.

# Orthographic Drawing Process

This process should help you when you are doing orthographic drawings.

1. Sketch out the views that you want in the correct places. Use the correct projection, first or third angle, sections or hidden details. This may involve sketching and measuring an actual object.

   If the final drawing is to have dimensions or other instructions, it is worth putting these on to your sketch drawing.

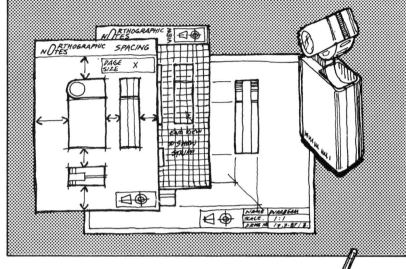

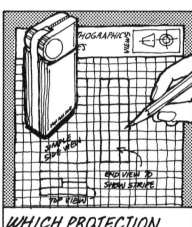

**WHICH PROJECTION AND WHICH VIEWS DO YOU NEED?**

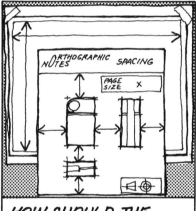

**HOW SHOULD THE VIEWS BE POSITIONED ON THE PAPER?**

**FAINTLY, DRAW THE VIEWS IN POSITION ON THE PAPER.**

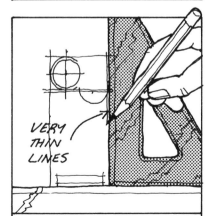

**FAINTLY, DRAW THE DETAILS OF THE OBJECT ON TO THE VIEWS.**

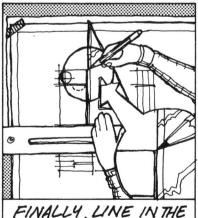

**FINALLY, LINE IN THE OBJECT MORE HEAVILY - BE VERY CAREFUL.**

2. Decide how the views should be placed on the paper. Space them sensibly so that you can easily see each one and the page is filled.

   It is not essential to space the views equally on the page, but this is a good habit to start with, so that you get used to the idea of spacing the views sensibly.

   Remember that the dimensions you need to describe an object may mean leaving extra space so that they can be fitted on.

# Orthographic Drawing   Third angle projection

You'll find that some people prefer first angle projection and some third angle. Third angle is used in America, first angle more in Britain and Europe. Try to think of it as a visual language and, as with spoken words, you can say things in different ways but still have the same meaning.

As with first angle projection the trick is to look straight on to the front/side and plan view of the object. Try not to think of the views having any perspective but as being like slides that are projected on to a flat screen.

For third angle projection imagine the object is laid on the page with its front view facing you. What you see on the left side you draw on the left of the front view and so on for the plan's other view.

3RD ANGLE PROJECTION- IMAGINE THE VIEWS ON A TRANSPARENT CUBE

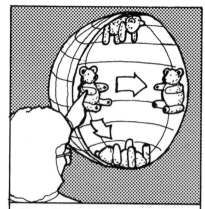

OR- THE OBJECT BEING SLID ON THE 'INSIDE' OF A HOLLOW SPHERE.

PRACTISE BY CONVERTING ISOMETRIC SKETCHES TO ORTHOGRAPHIC VIEWS.

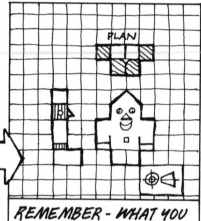

PLAN

REMEMBER - WHAT YOU SEE FROM ABOVE IS DRAWN ABOVE.

DESIGN A GAME WHERE YOU DRAW ISOMETRIC AND ORTHOGRAPHIC VIEWS

-OR DRAW OUT THE VIEWS- YOU THEN HAVE TO PUT THEM IN THE 'RIGHT' PLACES.

Practise becoming fluent with first and third angle projections by devising a game where you have to match the orthographic views of an object to an isometric drawing, and place the views in the correct places.

# Orthographic Drawing    Isometric to orthographic

One of the easiest ways of practising the skills of:

1. seeing objects in your head;
2. becoming familiar with orthographic views of objects;

is to work between isometric and orthographic drawings. Use grid and squared paper, and devise a game to test your understanding.

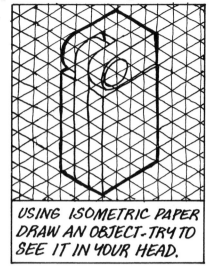

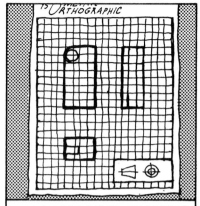

USING ISOMETRIC PAPER DRAW AN OBJECT - TRY TO SEE IT IN YOUR HEAD.

NOW IMAGINE TURNING THE OBJECT AROUND. DRAW THE THREE VIEWS.

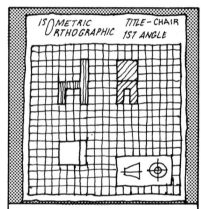

COLOUR IN THE FACES OF THE OBJECT (FRONT, SIDE, PLAN) DIFFERENTLY.

MAKE SURE YOU KNOW WHERE THE VIEWS WILL BE PLACED.

DRAW THE ORTHOGRAPHIC VIEWS ON TO SQUARED PAPER.

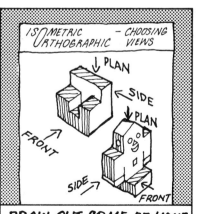

Also practise the process the other way round – that of drawing an isometric sketch from orthographic views. Other techniques of matching missing views, or adding missing details of views can be incorporated into the same game.

PRACTISE WORKING FROM ORTHOGRAPHIC TO ISOMETRIC VIEWS.

DRAW OUT SOME OF YOUR OWN EXAMPLES, SWAP THEM WITH A FRIEND.

# Orthographic Drawing views

# Transferring information between

Part of the fluency with orthographic drawing comes from placing and locating particular points on the other views. This example shows the technique of placing the position of the butterfly that has landed on the tent, in the front, side and plan views.

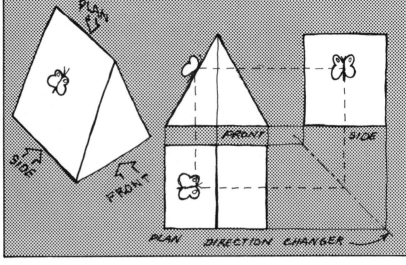

Look carefully at the technique of plotting from two of the views on to the third, to give the position on the plan view. This example shows the problem of drawing the plan view of the tent, and of placing the sloping edges in the plan view by projecting from the side and front views.

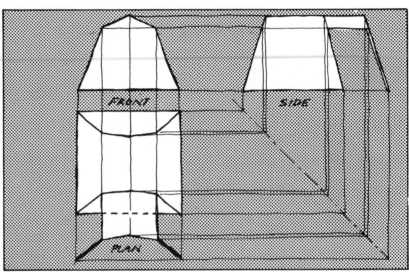

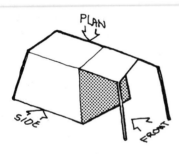

Devise a small project by taking a building and describing the outside of it as both orthographic and isometric drawings. Sketch the building first and then draw it out carefully, putting in as many of the external details as you feel necessary.

In order to be able to use orthographic drawings in their more complex situations it is essential that you become fluent with this technique.

PRODUCE ISOMETRIC AND ORTHOGRAPHIC DRAWINGS OF A BUILDING.

## References

All of the projects can involve orthographic drawings; they are designed so that you can practise these techniques.

**BS 308** is a booklet produced by the British Standards Association to make sure that there is a consistent drawing language. If you have any doubts you should get access to a copy of it.

# Orthographic Drawing   Cutting and sectioning, hidden detail

On orthographic drawings you have to find ways of showing details of the objects that are hidden, either because they are at the back of or inside the object.

The techniques are:

1. To use dotted lines to show hidden details of all sorts.
2. To take cross-sections which show the insides of the object.

These are both ways of showing similar things. To avoid confusion you don't normally put both of them on to the same view.

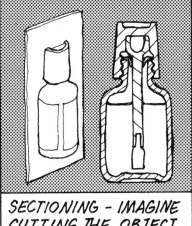

SECTIONING - IMAGINE CUTTING THE OBJECT IN HALF.

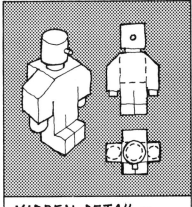

HIDDEN DETAIL - IMAGINE THE OBJECT IS MADE OF GLASS.

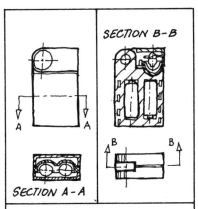

SECTION B-B

SECTION A - A

SHOW THE PLACE WHERE YOU SECTION THE OBJECT LIKE THIS.

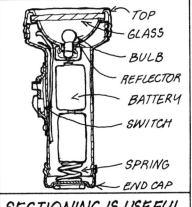

TOP
GLASS
BULB
REFLECTOR
BATTERY
SWITCH
SPRING
END CAP

SECTIONING IS USEFUL FOR SHOWING HOW THINGS FIT TOGETHER.

## Sectioning

You can section an object in any place and at any angle. The place where you have imagined the object cut is shown with a dash and dot line, and labels, as in the picture.

Sections are always used to make things clearer so choose the place for your section **carefully.**

Cut pieces are shown with diagonal lines, as in the picture.

DOTTED LINES SHOW THE HIDDEN DETAILS OF THIS CLOTHES PEG.

## Hidden detail

A good way of deciding whether a hidden detail should be shown or not, is to imagine that the object is made from glass. If you would see a line as you look *through* the object, then show a dotted line.

Dotted lines are shown like this:

— — — — — — — — — — — —

not like this:

. . . . . . . . . . . . . . . . . .

## References

There are certain rules about sectioning and hidden detail that it is important that you get correct. Many of them are in the section on engineering drawing, but BS 308 is the ultimate guide.

# Orthographic Drawing   Dimensioning

Dimensioning means putting sizes on to drawings.
These are the basic rules.

1. Keep things clear and uncomplicated.
2. Use the correct 'style' of letters and numbers.
3. Numbers and letters should be read from the **bottom** and the **right** only.
4. Only put on as many dimensions as you need to be able to draw, and eventually make, the object.
5. Keep the dimensions as clear of the outline of the object as possible.
6. Make sure that you are using the correct way of showing instructions and sizes.

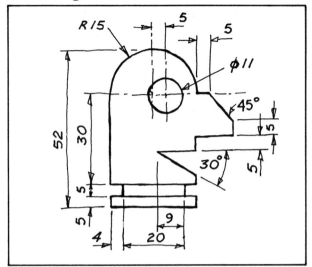

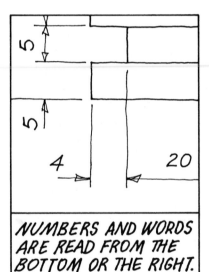

NUMBERS AND WORDS ARE READ FROM THE BOTTOM OR THE RIGHT.

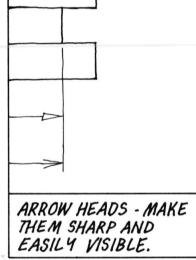

ARROW HEADS - MAKE THEM SHARP AND EASILY VISIBLE.

STENCIL
HANDWRITTEN
*CARTOON*
*123456789*

USE A SIMPLE, CAPITALS ONLY, WRITING STYLE. AVOID CONFUSION.

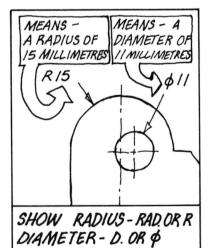

SHOW RADIUS - RAD. OR R
DIAMETER - D. OR ø

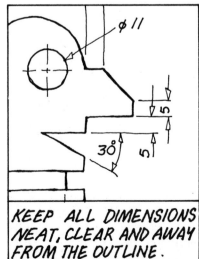

KEEP ALL DIMENSIONS NEAT, CLEAR AND AWAY FROM THE OUTLINE.

## References

Because it is like a language, dimensioning can always be improved, or shown in a different way. BS 308 is the best guide of what is acceptable. In the last resort, if it is clear and easy to understand, then it is probably acceptable.

# Development Nets and Packaging

This is about drawing something as a flattened out or unfolded shape. The objects are normally considered to be made from sheet material. Packages and models often have extra pieces that allow them to be glued together (called **tabs**).

You will find that although this is a simple idea, it is often quite difficult to do successfully. Always work carefully and measure and plot as accurately as you can.

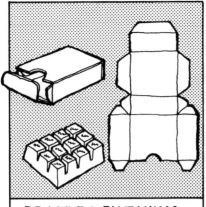

PRACTISE BY TAKING PACKAGES APART AND DRAWING THE SHAPE.

DRAW OUT AND MAKE A MODEL OF A BUILDING FROM FLAT CARD.

DEVELOPMENT OF A CYLINDER CUT AT AN ANGLE

IMAGINE DRAWING EQUALLY SPACED LINES AROUND THE OUTSIDE OF AN OBJECT, AND THEN UNWRAPPING IT ONE SECTION AT A TIME.

When dealing with complicated shapes, divide the object into smaller pieces that make it easier to understand. The cylindrical object on the left is split into twelve equal pieces, and then unrolled one section at a time. If you need to draw the flattened-out shape of a cylinder that has been cut at an angle, measure the length of each section as you unroll it.

The same technique is used with conical shapes - dividing up the outside, and unrolling the cone one section at a time.

## References

- Geometry      98–100
- Model making      63–5
- Packaging      18–19

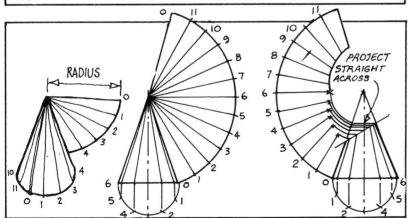

USE THE SAME PRINCIPLE, BUT THIS OBJECT IS CONICAL. NOTICE HOW THE HEIGHT OF THE CONE BECOMES THE RADIUS OF THE FLATTENED SHAPE.

# Systems Design/Flow Charts

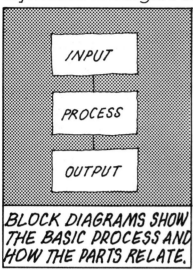

BLOCK DIAGRAMS SHOW THE BASIC PROCESS AND HOW THE PARTS RELATE.

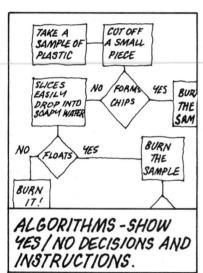

ALGORITHMS - SHOW YES/NO DECISIONS AND INSTRUCTIONS.

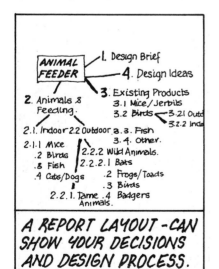

A REPORT LAYOUT - CAN SHOW YOUR DECISIONS AND DESIGN PROCESS.

The skill of being able to show projects and ideas as diagrams and charts is an important ability for you to develop as a designer.

The simplest way of showing a process is that of an input/output system. An input to the system is processed and causes an output.

Brainstorming is a technique where you write on to cards all the things that you can think of about a certain design problem. Then try to classify them into similar areas. This not only helps you to think about what is missing, but can also give you ideas about possible answers.

Algorithms are drawn to show a process as a series of statements to which the answer is either yes or no. These charts are the basis of most computer programming.

Spider diagrams use the idea of starting from one basic object and trying to relate information to it (like branches on a tree). This is also a good note-taking method where it is important to record the connections between things as well as the facts.

A designer would normally write out a summary of the project, including the research, ideas, decisions and argument which led to the final design. This is known as a design report. You could write one yourself. It is a good way of sorting out your ideas and explaining them to someone else.

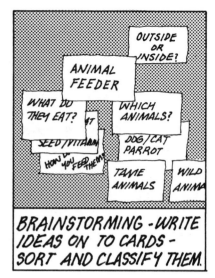

BRAINSTORMING - WRITE IDEAS ON TO CARDS - SORT AND CLASSIFY THEM.

SPIDER DIAGRAMS - FOR NOTE TAKING AND FOR SHOWING THE LINKS.

# Model Making

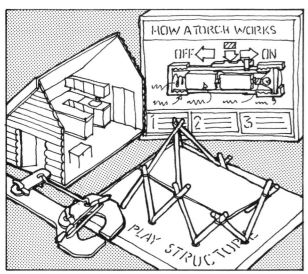

Much of designing involves getting vague ideas out of your head and into reality, so that others can understand what you are talking about. Models are a valuable tool in this process.

Beware of the words 'rough model'. As with drawings think and plan first, then make the models as carefully as you can. Always try things out before you use them on your models. Try to use the same technique as in a paste-up where you avoid the casual error to one small piece which ruins the whole thing.

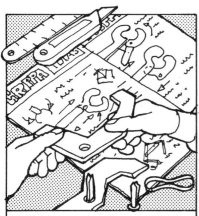

CHOOSE THE KIND OF MODEL - REMEMBER WHO - WHY - WHAT.

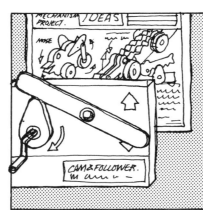

IS IT TO WORK OUT YOUR OWN IDEAS, OR TO SHOW TO SOMEONE ELSE?

IS IT TO BE A COPY OF THE FINAL DESIGN FOR THE 'CLIENT'?

PLAN THE MODEL FIRST. TRY OUT THE DIFFICULT PARTS.

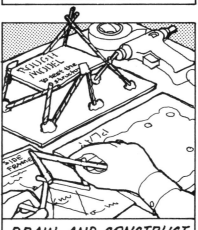

DRAW AND CONSTRUCT THE MODEL WITH EXTREME CARE.

LOOK AT YOUR FINISHED WORK, HOW GOOD IS IT? COULD IT BE BETTER?

# Model Making   Tools and materials

The range of materials that you can use will depend on the range of facilities that you have and also what you are good at. Remember that the tools you use can be dangerous. Always act sensibly and try to avoid damaging yourself and others.

You will be aware that certain paints and glues can give off fumes which can be dangerous. Always take great care to read the instructions on materials and avoid any that could be harmful to you or others.

PAPER AND CARD, SCISSORS, CUTTING KNIVES, GLUE.

Many of the normal school workshop materials can be used for model making. A few simple tools plus a place to work will normally be sufficient for quite complicated models.

Professional model makers often have quite limited facilities, but they make up for this with an **enormous** amount of carefulness.

Experiment with different materials like foam plastics and pre-prepared kits, to see what tricks you can develop to make your models look finished. Often the addition of a 'bought in' piece to a fairly sketchy model can give it a more impressive look.

WOOD - FOR SMALLER PIECES USE A SAW AND GLASSPAPER FOR SHAPING

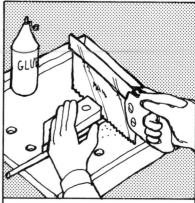

FIND SOMEWHERE TO WORK. DON'T DAMAGE TABLE SURFACES.

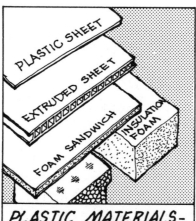

PLASTIC MATERIALS - STRIPS, FOAM, SPECIAL SHEETS AND EXTRUSIONS.

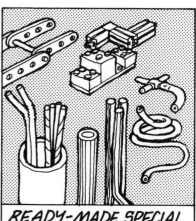

READY-MADE SPECIAL MATERIALS, STRAWS, KITS, TUBES, FITTINGS.

# Safety and Storage

Probably the most dangerous things you will use when model making will be sharp knives. The knives have to be sharp or they won't work properly.

1. Use a safety ruler.
2. Put the ruler on the side of the piece of material that you want, so that if you slip you won't ruin the good bit.
3. Always cut on a cutting mat or on some substance that won't blunt the knife or mark the table top.

Be very careful painting and finishing your models. It is very easy to ruin a lot of hard work with carelessness. Never think that paint will hide the faults, it is more likely to make them worse. It may be better to finish and paint the pieces of your models first and then put them together.

Finished models are always quite delicate. After your initial presentation, it is a good idea to either photograph them or make some kind of storage box to keep them in.

*BE VERY CAREFUL WITH CUTTING KNIVES - USE A SAFETY RULER.*

Be prepared to use any kinds of tricks and clever materials available to you, for example:

- Hot glue guns
- Velcro tape
- Double sided tape
- Press studs
- Any other kinds of fasteners that will make things easier for you, yet look good.

*MAKE A SPECIAL STORAGE BOX OR TAKE A SERIES OF PHOTOGRAPHS OF YOUR FINISHED MODEL.*

*ADD THE FINAL DETAILS WITH CARE. AVOID MISTAKES, SAVE TIME.*

## References

# Presentation Principles

Most drawings have two main functions:

1. To get an idea out of your head so that you can look at it.
2. To tell someone else something.

Really the two are the same but drawings done for yourself can be less precise, whereas for someone else you will need a more detailed presentation. The idea is to use the techniques in this book for both of these jobs, but only use as much presentation as you think is useful and that you have the time for.

**Remember**, whilst they may be beautiful, never attempt to produce works of art. A good and careful drawing is just as effective as an elaborately coloured illustration.

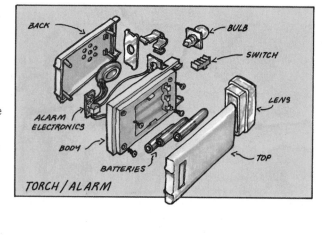

The drawing and the presentation are done to **communicate** something. Simplicity can often get the message across far better than complexity. Often, what look like simple drawings, have had a lot of thought and effort put into them.

Always practise techniques before using them on your drawings. Get to know the range of things that work for you, and learn where the difficulties arise. The sequence I have used for producing the drawings in this book has been:

1. Sketch drawings, with notes on who it is for, and the kind of drawing.
2. Doing the first drawing carefully and faintly, checking scale and details.
3. Correcting the first drawing. Ruling in straight lines and drawing circles with a compass.
4. Turning the drawing over and checking and correcting it from the back. (This should show up mistakes in perspective.)
5. Redrawing or tracing the drawing on to a new piece of paper.
6. Finally reducing/copying/ mounting/and adding colour and shade.

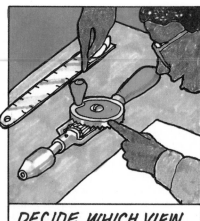

DECIDE WHICH VIEW OF THE OBJECT YOU WANT AND WHY.

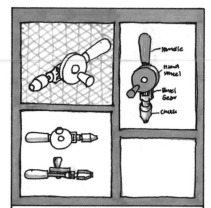

CHOOSE THE TECHNIQUE THAT YOU FIND EASIEST TO WORK WITH.

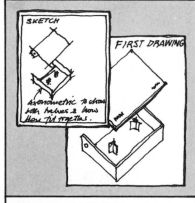

PLAN, SKETCH, AND DRAW OUT THE OBJECT.

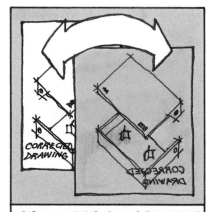

CHECK THE PERSPECTIVE. DRAW IN STRAIGHT LINES AND CIRCLES.

# Presentation Principles

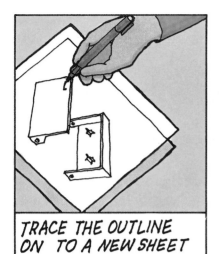

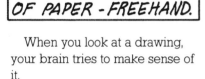

**TRACE THE OUTLINE ON TO A NEW SHEET OF PAPER - FREEHAND.**

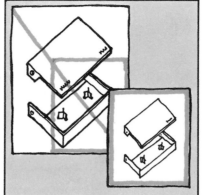

**REDUCE THE DRAWING TO ITS FINAL, CORRECT SIZE.**

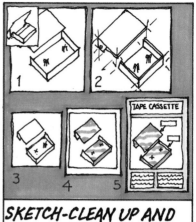

**SKETCH-CLEAN UP AND CORRECT-TRACE-REDUCE -COLOUR/SHADE-PASTE UP.**

When you look at a drawing, your brain tries to make sense of it.

One of the best clues the brain has for working things out is in noting which object is in front of the other. The technique on the right uses a thick line to show which edges of a drawing have a space behind them. Thin lines are used for all other edges.

Learn this rule and then try it out by tracing an existing drawing, and checking that it works.

Coloured outlines around drawings have the same effect: that of separating the drawings from the background and making them 'stand out'. Don't use too dark a colour for the outline or it might look ridiculous.

Cutting out the drawing and mounting it on to different coloured paper can have the same effect.

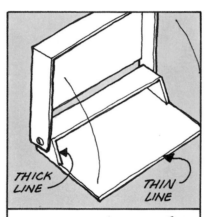

**DRAW ALL OF THE OBJECT IN THIN LINES - ADD THE THICK LINES LATER.**

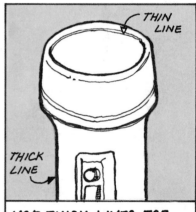

**USE THICK LINES FOR OUTLINES AND TO SHOW EDGES IN FRONT OF OTHERS.**

Start collecting illustrations from books or magazines that you like. (See if you can work out how they are done.) Collect examples or illustrations of things that you find difficult, like hands or chrome, or other materials.

**SHADED OUTLINES MAKE THE IMAGE STAND OUT FROM THE BACKGROUND.**

# Shading

What you should try to do is to keep the drawing as simple as possible then add as little shading, colour and line as possible. Use these extra techniques to **add** to a good drawing rather than to disguise a poor one. There is no alternative to looking and drawing carefully.

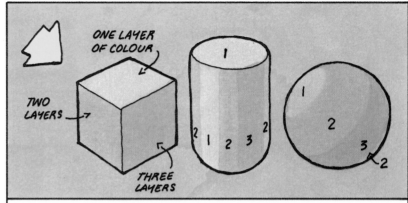

IMAGINE THAT THE LIGHT IS COMING FROM THE TOP LEFT. YOU CAN DESCRIBE AN OBJECT USING THREE TONES OR THREE THIN LAYERS OF COLOUR.

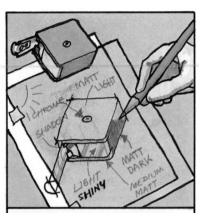

SKETCH THE OBJECT - DECIDE WHERE THE LIGHT AND DARK PARTS ARE.

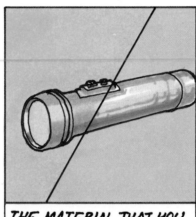

THE MATERIAL THAT YOU ARE REPRESENTING MAY BE MATT OR SHINY.

YOU MAY CHOOSE TO REPRESENT THE OBJECT ONLY USING LINES.

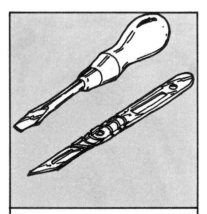

EVEN IF YOU USE BLACK LINES TO SHOW LIGHT BITS, IT WILL STILL WORK.

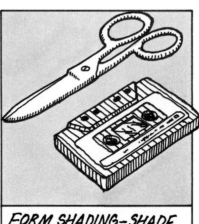

FORM SHADING-SHADE LINES WHICH FOLLOW THE OBJECT'S SHAPE.

Work out in advance where the light and dark parts will be. Always remember that what you are trying to do is to give a person enough clues so that they can understand what you have drawn. Don't shade everything in. It is better to put on just a little shading that doesn't confuse the reader, than too much.

# Colour

As with shading, use colour sparingly for the best effect. Work out in advance, and rehearse if necessary, the techniques you are going to use. Try to use the techniques which you feel confident with, to produce both the effect that you want and also to be able to correct it if you get it wrong.

Collect examples of bits of technique, and effects that you like, try to copy them and then incorporate them into your work.

CHALK IS USED TO SHOW THE LIGHT AND DARK AREAS, CRAYON IS ADDED TO REPRESENT THE PARTICULAR MATERIAL. NOTICE HOW LITTLE YOU NEED!

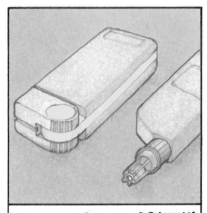

THIS IS A PENCIL DRAWING SHADED WITH A SPIRIT BASED FELT MARKER.

AN INK DRAWING WITH WATER BASED FELT PEN. NOTE THE DIFFERENCE.

## References

Try to experiment and add shading and colour to all of your sketches. You have to practise looking at objects, drawing them and noticing where the light and shaded parts are. Then develop your own techniques of showing the objects.

THIN COATS OF COLOUR CAN BE PUT ON WITH WATER COLOUR PAINTS.

SPRAYED OR SPLATTERED PAINT GIVES GENTLE COLOUR CHANGES.

# Ellipses in Graphics

When you look at a circular object from an angle you see an ellipse. Your brain is used to seeing ellipses and knowing that they are really circular.

These are a few tips on how to draw ellipses:

1. Draw in the minor axis.
2. Make sure that the major axis is 90° to it.
3. Now sketch an ellipse.
4. Correct it and line it in more heavily.

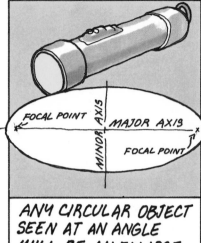
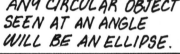

ANY CIRCULAR OBJECT SEEN AT AN ANGLE WILL BE AN ELLIPSE.

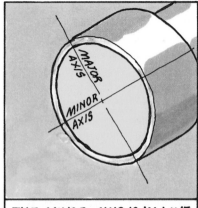

THE MINOR AXIS IS IN LINE WITH THE HOLE, THE MAJOR AXIS IS AT 90° TO IT.

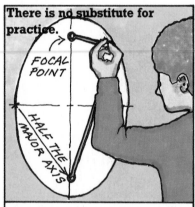

DRAW AN ELLIPSE - TWO PINS (AT THE FOCAL POINTS) AND A LOOP OF STRING.

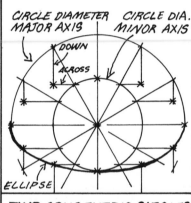

TWO CONCENTRIC CIRCLES
1. THE MAJOR AXIS.
2. THE MINOR AXIS.

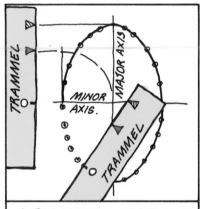

A TRAMMEL - KEEP THE ARROWS ON THE MAJOR AND MINOR AXES.

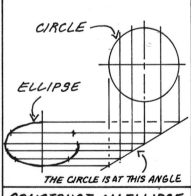

CONSTRUCT AN ELLIPSE FROM A CIRCLE AT AN ANGLE.

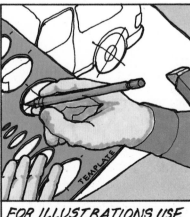

FOR ILLUSTRATIONS USE ELLIPSE TEMPLATES. LINE UP THE MINOR AXES

You need to practise drawing things so that you can see the ellipses and their axes in your head before you draw them.

**There is no substitute for practice.**

## References

- Geometry                98–9
- Most project work will involve ellipses in some form

# Exploded Drawing

Exploded drawings require a combination of several skills. They are a pictorial way of describing the pieces of a particular object and how they fit together. The pieces are arranged as though they were about to fit together, or as if they have just exploded and are moving apart.

Perspective exploded drawings can be quite difficult to get right. It is often easier to use one of the picturing techniques that uses plan or front views (page 51) to simplify the actual drawing.

Make sure that you have an accurate record of how the pieces fit together before you start an exploded drawing.

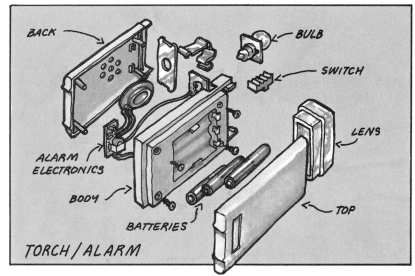

TORCH / ALARM

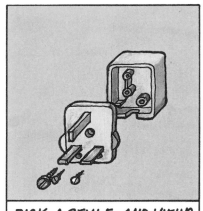

PICK A STYLE AND VIEWS TO SIMPLIFY THE DRAWING YET SHOW THE DETAILS.

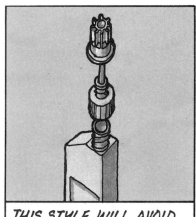

THIS STYLE WILL AVOID HAVING TO DRAW ELLIPSES YET STILL 'WORKS'.

TAKE THE OBJECT APART, MAKE DETAILED NOTES BEFORE YOU DRAW IT.

Remember that the purpose of the drawing is to show the pieces and how they fit together. The drawing must be clear and accurate.

# Some Professional Designers' Work

**Phill Rooke** is a sculptor. He works as a sculptor in residence at the Islington Sixth-Form Centre. Phill believes that his work should involve people, so his work is not only about people and their reactions to the technological world they live in, people are also involved in the designing and making of the sculpture.

Phill discusses his work at all stages and the ideas are changed because of his and other people's feelings about it. You can see (left) his process from stimulus material through to a full-sized drawing, and then the carving he made from the drawing. The carving follows the final drawing closely.

**Jo Compton** is a knitwear designer. Her starting point is what she calls the 'feel' that she wants for the final product. In this case (bottom left) it is an 'overgarment'. She says her stimulus comes from lots of places: from objects like stones and feathers, from garments and fashion styles and from experimenting with different yarns.

Her original experimental knitting sample led her to put down, as ideas, how the design could be used. Once the final idea was chosen, she worked out the sizes and shapes of the pieces needed. She then knitted and sewed together the final garment.

**Ken Lumsden** is the production manager for the Habitat catalogue. When he is designing the catalogue he has two basic briefs:

1. That he is primarily selling an image or life-style. 'When you buy one of the products, you are buying into a way of life.'

# Some Professional Designers' Work

**2.** To display a range of products that have been bought and manufactured by the company.

The previous catalogue is discussed and any general changes in feeling and image decided.

Ken and his team then plan and draw each page, showing the products and the settings they will be in. These drawings go to the photographers and the set builders. Ken says that the set builders sometimes need a plan drawing, but not always. The details of the text go to the typographer.

The whole set is constructed and photographed, with discussions and modifications, and then the final page is put together for printing. Notice (top right) the similarity between the sketch and the actual picture.

**Alan Colville** is a graphic designer for Ian Logan Designs. When he designed the soap wrapper (right), he had two basic briefs:

**1.** To design something that was simple, and different to traditional soap wrappings.

**2.** To be cheap and simple to produce by silk screen printing.

He had the idea of using folded paper with an oriental feeling and experimented with pieces of paper to see how they could be made to lock together without needing glue.

The graphics were designed to be printed in four colours only, so that they would give an impact both singly and in multiples. The shop counter display was then designed to echo the feeling of the product graphics.

# Some Professional Designers' Work

**Adrian Stokes, David Banham** and **Stuart Lambert** are all designers for ASA. They were approached to design an information terminal, for use in shops and exhibitions etc. The inventor had already made a prototype of his idea (near right), but they decided that it needed to be rethought so that it would be easier to produce and use. The major changes were to alter the position of the unit to a traditional typing position, and to introduce a LCD display and a flat membrane keyboard.

They produced a series of sketch ideas which were made into foam models (near right) so that they could see what their ideas looked like. Once they had satisfied themselves that the idea looked as though it would work, accurate scale drawings were made and from these the first model was made.

In discussion with the client it was decided that the terminal looked too hard and unfriendly. They then modified their design to the final version. Detail drawings of the parts of the terminal were then produced, for the manufacture of the pieces.

**Richard Miles** is a product designer for Fether and Partners. Richard and his team have designed a new range of suitcases for Samsonite. A range of early ideas were produced as sketches and foam models, and these were then translated into pictorial drawings. These were discussed with the client company and a certain style chosen.

Design features of the whole range are:

# Some Professional Designers' Work

1. An injection moulded construction.
2. Non identical top and bottom halves.
3. Wheels and wheel handles on all of the range.

The actual shape and sizes of the different-sized cases in the range were developed, and tested out as foam models (the cases should fit inside each other). The details and design of the wheels, catches and handles were drawn out as detail drawings and made up in full-sized model form. The drawings for the manufacture of the suitcases were then drawn out by Samsonite in Belgium.

**Isherwood and Co.** are interior designers. They were asked to produce designs for Lifestyle, a chain of health food shops. The designs were to include the whole image of the shops from the design of the shops to the packaging of the goods.

Jon Isherwood and Tony Whitehead worked initially on the ideas and the concept. They found that it was very easy to say what the image shouldn't be. So they started from scratch with ideas like – what is the origin of life? The sun, the earth and the air? Tony's drawings show the development of the **logo,** and Jon's sketch shows how the colour scheme and feeling could be used on the shopfront. The rest of the pictures helped to present their ideas to the client.

Detailed shopfitting drawings were then produced for each shop. A directory was compiled showing how the basic formula should be applied to packaging and signs. This enables the client to organise their production.

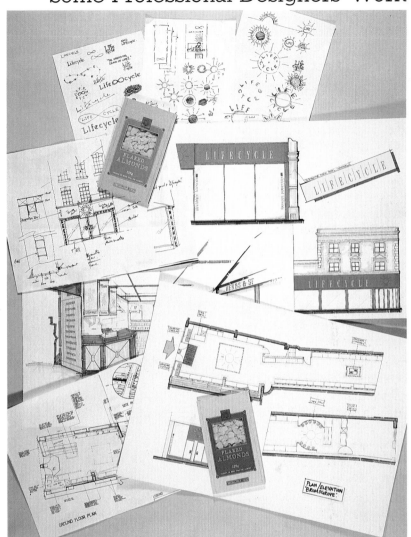

# Engineering Drawing Principles

Engineering drawings are used by the designer to communicate with the manufacturer. The rules about the way information is presented are included in BS 308. Different people and manufacturers will have different standards, but always within the BS 308 guidelines. The reasons for such strict standards are:

**1.** To make sure the object is made correctly.
**2.** To avoid costly mistakes.
**3.** To avoid confusion, and waste of time.

The number and kinds of drawings needed will depend on:

**1.** How complicated the object is.
**2.** How important it is if it is made wrongly.
**3.** The number of people involved.

All of the drawings on this page have been made into objects.

It is important not to just draw things but to work out what the drawing will mean to the person who makes the object. They may use the drawing to work out the easiest and cheapest way of making the object.

Try to think and plan for the person who will be making the object, and make sure that they will find it easy to understand.

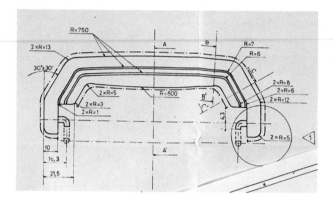

# Engineering Drawing Principles

An engineering drawing should also contain all the information that the person following it will need.

When you have decided who the drawing is for and what they will need, plan out the way the drawing will be laid out, and the general details and information that need to go on it. Try to avoid getting half way through the drawing and realising that you've chosen the wrong scale.

**MAKE DETAILED NOTES OF WHAT EACH PERSON'S NEEDS ARE.**

**TALK TO PEOPLE TO FIND OUT WHAT THEY NEED FROM YOUR DRAWINGS.**

## Nuts and bolts

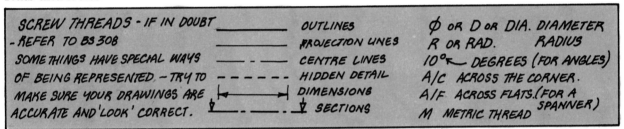

SCREW THREADS - IF IN DOUBT - REFER TO BS 308

SOME THINGS HAVE SPECIAL WAYS OF BEING REPRESENTED. - TRY TO MAKE SURE YOUR DRAWINGS ARE ACCURATE AND 'LOOK' CORRECT.

———— OUTLINES
———— PROJECTION LINES
—— - —— CENTRE LINES
- - - - - - HIDDEN DETAIL
|←————→| DIMENSIONS
SECTIONS

ϕ or D or DIA. DIAMETER
R or RAD.  RADIUS
10° DEGREES (FOR ANGLES)
A/C ACROSS THE CORNER.
A/F ACROSS FLATS. (FOR A SPANNER)
M METRIC THREAD

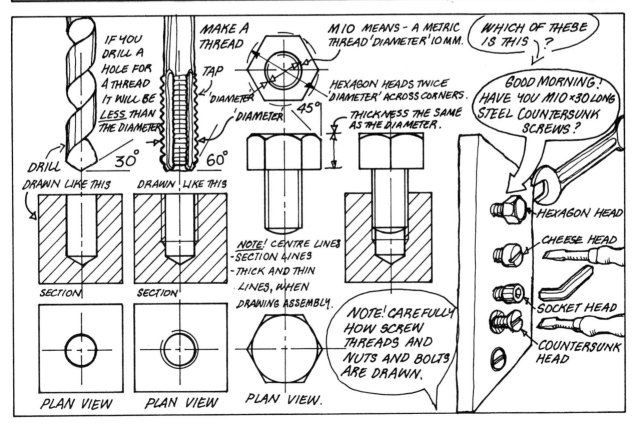

# Engineering Drawing Principles

The conventions (rules) of engineering drawing also apply for most other drawings of objects that are to be made. There may be slightly different ways of showing things, but providing that you stick to BS 308 you cannot go far wrong.

Engineers often talk about being able to 'read' a drawing. This means that they can look at the drawing and understand the object that it represents – not only the sizes and shape of it – but how you, the designer, intended it to be made.

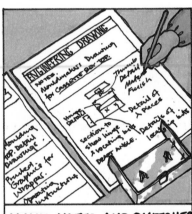

**MAKE NOTES AND SKETCHES OF THE THINGS YOU NEED TO SHOW IN YOUR DRAWING.**

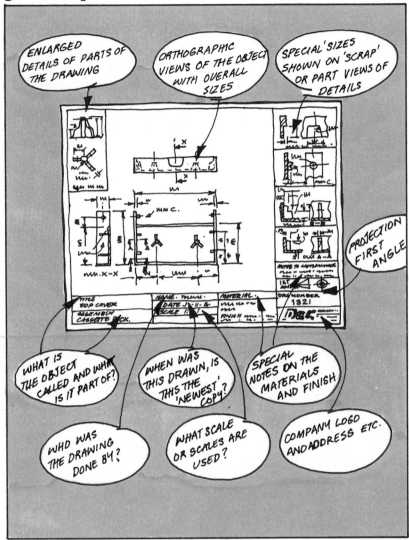

Whilst the general rules of orthographic projection will be sufficient to show the object, it is worth checking with the appropriate British Standards that you are representing things correctly.

| British Standards | Title |
|---|---|
| BS 308 | Engineering Drawing Practice |
| BS 1192 | Building Drawing Practice |
| PD 7308 | Engineering Drawing for Schools and Colleges |
| PD 7307 | Graphical Symbols for Use in Schools and Colleges |
| BS 4058 | Data Processing Flow Chart Symbols Rules and Conventions |

When you are designing something you will probably do several quick orthographic views of the object in pencil. From this you will take all the other drawings of the object. But since the pencil drawings are for yourself only, you need not follow all the rules of engineering drawing.

# Engineering Drawing Principles    Assembly Drawing

Assembly drawings are often cross-sections of the entire object, showing how the pieces fit together, what they are called and what they are made from.

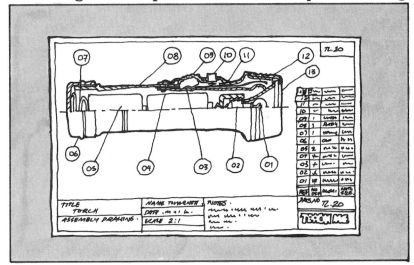

1. Sections should always be used to make things **easier** to understand. Do not combine section lines and (dotted) hidden detail on the same view. You do not section nuts, bolts, washers, shafts, pins and webs. Draw them as though they are seen from the outside and not cut. Check with BS 308 if you are in any doubt.

2. Label each of the pieces with a number reference. Take care to keep numbers, dimensions and lettering **away** from the drawing outline.

3. Think about who will use the parts' list and what information they will need. Do they need information about materials or is that on a detail drawing? – in which case they need to know the drawing number of the detail drawing.

This is a way that you can practise assembly drawing with another person.

1. Draw a section through an assembly of an object.

2. From this draw the sections of the individual pieces.

3. The other person now has to cut out and paste back together the details.

4. Finally trace the complete assembly drawing.

DRAW OUT SECTIONAL VIEWS OF THE PIECES OF THE OBJECT.

YOUR PARTNER NOW HAS TO RE-ASSEMBLE THE OBJECT AS DRAWINGS.

# Engineering Drawing Principles   Detail drawing

Detail drawings should contain all the information that the maker needs to manufacture that particular object.

1. Views so that they can understand what the object is.
2. Sizes and special features like screw threads, so that such a piece will fit the object.
3. Details of how it is to be made and from what materials.
4. How it is to be finished (polished, painted, cleaned).
5. How many objects are to be made.

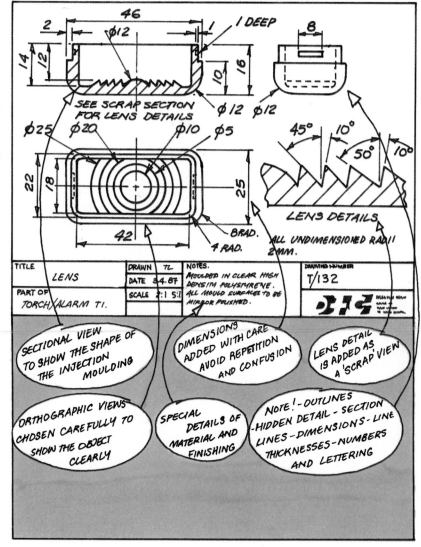

Computer draughting can simplify the process of generating and producing detail drawings by being able to take detail drawings directly from scale models or assembly drawings. The advantage of this technique, apart from saving time, is that mistakes made on the detail drawings which may mean that the object won't fit together, will be avoided.

# Computer Graphics

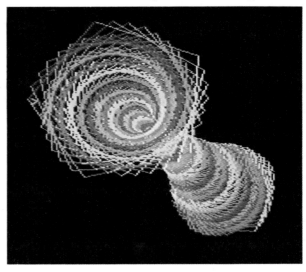

**Teachers' note** It would be impossible to give a general and meaningful guide to computer graphics because all the brands of computer are slightly different even though their operating principles are the same. In addition, the amount of software available is expanding rapidly, with each one capable of doing more complex and sophisticated things.

The computer graphics option within the syllabus is dependent on you having the correct equipment. At present what is required in this option is pretty basic in computing terms, but may always be a minority option because of the facilities that a school will need in order to provide it for a whole group of students.

If you do have the correct equipment, there is no substitute for experience and time spent computing. But if you do not, there are many things that a computer can do which students might find useful at other points in the course, e.g. word processing, data bases and charting and graphing programs.

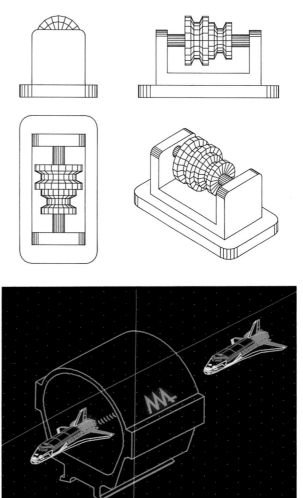

# Computer Graphics

As can be seen from current television programmes the use of computer graphics is enormous. Be aware, however, that the computer graphics you do at this level cannot match the sophistication of what you see on the television.

The starting point with producing pictures is to imagine that the screen is a large piece of graph paper. You then place dots on this 'graph paper' and join up the dots with straight or curved lines.

You can either work out the positions of the dots as numbers and put them into the computer via the keyboard, or you can use a digitiser. As you can imagine, even quite a simple picture can take a long time to create.

More sophisticated than this is to use the computer's ability to repeat calculations very quickly. By setting up a basic calculation which produces two dots and then repeating this many times you can develop quite complex patterns.

Animating and creating graphics that can be changed in scale can be a great advantage. This 'anthropometrics' aid (bottom picture) was developed using LOGO. If you insert the measurements of the person you are designing something for, the animated figure will assume these measurements. You can then manipulate the figure to sit, reach or kneel etc., in order to help you to design equipment for a specific person.

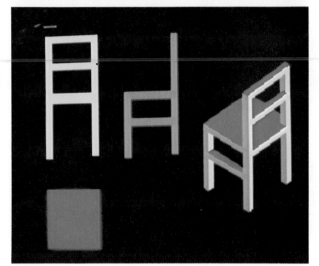

# Computer Graphics

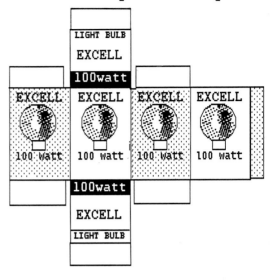

With the increasing sophistication of software has come the ability to shortcut many of the graphics.

## General graphics package

This type of software can produce a wide range of text, graphics and paste-up facilities, as well as repeat and mirror facilities. The illustration on the right shows an example of its use in designing the package and graphics for a packaging product. The particular facilities used were the ability to create and vary the size of the package. (In this program I had to print and fold up the packages to test out how they looked. The designers' package software explained below allows me to fold them up without printing them out.)

## Three-dimensional designers' package

This type of software is a sophisticated designing, visualising and drawing tool. Objects can be created on the screen, modified (manufactured) then converted to engineering drawings with dimensions and other instructions. Components can be assembled and separated; folded shapes can be constructed, and machining processes like extrusion can be simulated.

It can replace much of the work done on orthographic drawing and the production of engineering drawings. It also enables you to modify drawings quickly and consistently.

The user **must** know what they want to end up with, so the skills of visualisation and rotating views are essential, but what you don't have to do is produce the drawings manually.

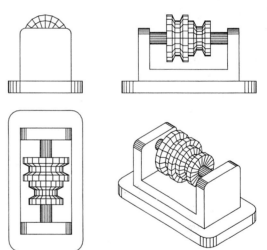

## Desk top publisher

Computer-generated publishing is widely used commercially and is now also possible with the range of smaller computers. The software allows a range of graphical techniques which combine text, pictures and headings in a newspaper format.

When communicating information in any kind of presentation this kind of software would be valuable. Mini project work can be presented in this form.

The software programmes are not cheap. Make sure you know what the package does and doesn't do and how reliable it is before you buy it.

### Philippine Ecumenical Network
P E N

Newsletter No. 1 November 1988

#### The Philippines Today

A revolution is a time for enmities to be put aside and alliances cemented wherever they can be found. It is a time for people to stop turning their backs on each other and going their own tragic and separate ways. It is also a time when those who have been excluded from the political and economic community because they are peasants or at least brought in and inherit their own land where they have been strangers. It is a time when all political, economic and social issues are to be subjected to a radical questioning which must ask, above all, why is it that the poor and powerless absorb in themselves, always, the sin of society as a whole.

When Marcos was overthrown in February 1986 the Filipino people hoped that the Aquino government

would begin to tackle these questions. Twenty months later all the signs are that the revolution has yet to happen. Aquino' accession to power fuelled high hopes of a freer society. She advocated reconciliation and made stirring calls for People Power. She became the symbol of the centre from which flowed all the solutions to Philippine problems. But now the people are not so sure. She is unsheathing the sword of war and has asked her army to give her a 'string of victories' against those who want radical solutions to the country's problems. The organised left and its sympathisers are categorised as terrorists.

*Extract from A Smouldering Land by Julian Eagle. Published by CIIR. 22 Coleman Fields, London N1 7AF. Price 85p + postage.*

#### The Role of the Churches

The Philippines is the only country in Asia where Christians form a majority of the population (85 per

the poor was imprisonment, harassment, torture and sometimes death. During the period 1974 to

the administration's 'total war' policy. Nuns, priests, pastors an deaconesses, who live and work wit

# Energy

You should be aware that energy is a constant property which can be changed from one form to another. The idea of energy being wasted really means that it has been changed into something that is not so useful; it doesn't actually disappear.

In the picture on the right energy is changed from uphill (potential) energy to movement (kinetic) energy when it falls, to sound and heat energy when it hits the table.

The cycle in the rest of the picture is chemical energy to heat energy to movement energy to electrical energy to light and heat energy.

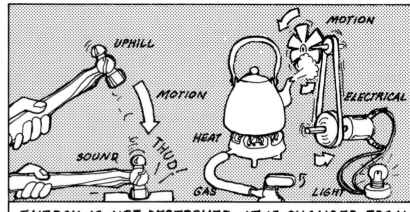

ENERGY IS NOT DESTROYED. IT IS CHANGED FROM ONE FORM TO ANOTHER.

DIFFERENT EQUIPMENT MAY MAKE THINGS EASIER TO DO.

You may be expected to show something in your project work about the uses of energy, and sources of energy, for example, coal, oil, gas and sunlight. The local issue project (pages 32–5) is designed to cover this area.

When you work you use up energy. Of the two people on bicycles, one is finding riding up the hill much easier than the other. Why do you think this is?
- Is it the person?
- Is it the difference between the bikes?

Which bike makes best use of the rider's energy?

**Location of power stations at 31 March 1987**

| | Declared net capability megawatts sent out | No. of stations |
|---|---|---|
| Coal-fired | 30 537 | 37 |
| Coal/gas-fired | 366 | 1 |
| Coal/oil-fired | 4 504 | 3 |
| Oil-fired | 6 775 | 7 |
| Nuclear | 5 029 | 10 |
| Gas-turbine | 1 442 | 11 |
| Hydro | 112 | 7 |
| Pumped-storage | 2 088 | 2 |
| Auxiliary gas-turbines | 1 510 | — |
| Total | 52 363 | 78 |

SOURCES OF ELECTRICITY (CEGB)

COAL FIRED
COAL/GAS FIRED + HYDRO
COAL/OIL FIRED
AUXILIARY GAS TURBINE
PUMPED STORAGE
GAS TURBINE
NUCLEAR
OIL FIRED

PRACTISE USING CHARTS AND DIAGRAMS TO COMPARE ENERGY SOURCES AND THE CONVERSION OF ENERGY TO OTHER FORMS.

# Electrics  Basics

You will not need to understand the complicated ideas involved in electricity, but you should be aware of the terms voltage, current and resistance. They are related by:

voltage = current × resistance

It may be easier to understand if you think of electricity like water. So that:

voltage = pressure
current = water flow
resistance = the size of the pipe

Practise representing electrical systems as diagrams. The torch shows the electrical circuit, the kettle shows it as a system diagram (this is a difficult example).

**Be extremely careful with any electrical equipment. Ask before you take things apart, and if you are in any doubt, don't do it.**

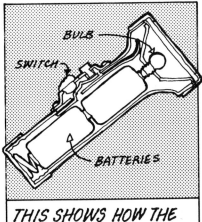

THIS SHOWS HOW THE TORCH FITS TOGETHER, BUT NOT HOW IT WORKS.

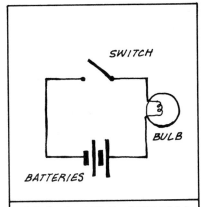

THIS IS THE ELECTRICAL CIRCUIT DIAGRAM FOR THE TORCH.

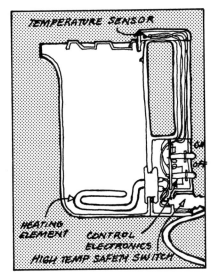

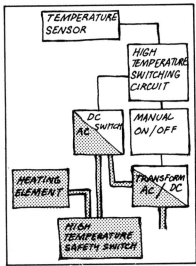

The diagram on the right shows a simple electronic circuit. The basic block diagram shows the stages of the circuit; the actual circuit represents the components diagramatically.

## References

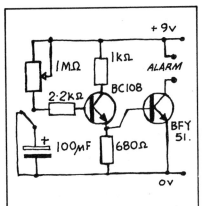

ELECTRONIC CIRCUIT DIAGRAM FOR A TIMER ALARM.

BLOCK DIAGRAM OF A TIMER ALARM.

# Electronics

| NAME | PICTURE | SYMBOL |
|------|---------|--------|
| RESISTOR | | 2.2 KΩ |
| TRANSISTOR | npn / pnp | BC108 |
| CAPACITOR | 10MF | 1MF / 0·01MF |
| LIGHT (LDR) DEPENDENT RESISTOR | | ORP 12 |

| NAME | PICTURE | SYMBOL |
|------|---------|--------|
| INTEGRATED CIRCUIT (MICROCHIP) | 555 | I.C.1 |
| DIODE | | |
| RELAY | | |
| MOTOR | | M |

Very few people actually design electronic circuits but you should be able to draw out the circuit diagrams and have an understanding of what the components do.

On the right is a simple thermostat circuit. When the temperature rises above a certain temperature the fan switches on. This is the same system as in most car radiator cooling fans.

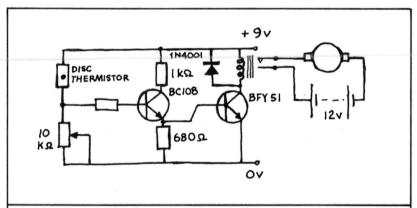

THIS CIRCUIT DIAGRAM SHOWS HOW THE COMPONENTS ARE ARRANGED TO WORK AS A THERMOSTATIC FAN. YOU NEED TO BE ABLE TO IDENTIFY THE COMPONENTS.

THE PROCESS OF MAKING A PRINTED CIRCUIT BOARD FROM A CIRCUIT DIAGRAM.

WORK OUT THE POSITIONS OF THE COMPONENTS - DRAW IN THE CONNECTIONS.

ETCH AWAY THE COPPER - LEAVING THE CONNECTIONS. SOLDER ON THE COMPONENTS.

# Structures and Materials

When you are building and making structures two of the basic things that you've got to consider are:

1. What you make it from.
2. How you shape or put the material together to give you the result that you want.

Choose the materials and types of structure which work best for the object you are making.

Many things are made from frame structures because they are light, efficient and cheap (see the photo). There are certain basic rules about frame structures (note the three examples in the diagram, right).

Card and paper structures have certain basic rules when you are making boxes and packages from them (these are mostly common sense).

1. Paper is very good in tension, but not very good at anything else.
2. You can get strength from paper and card by the way that you fold, or double up the thickness.
3. You can use curved creases and folds to your advantage.

Certain materials are only good in one way, for example concrete is good in compression but cracks if loaded any other way. Rope is only any good in tension. Rubber is good at twisting. It is stretchy and will shape in a way that allows it to shape easily (like an elastic band).

This crane is a typical frame structure. Notice the triangular frames which give it its strength.

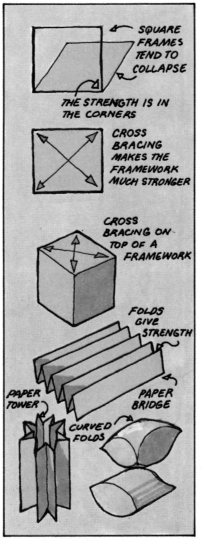

SQUARE FRAMES TEND TO COLLAPSE

THE STRENGTH IS IN THE CORNERS

CROSS BRACING MAKES THE FRAMEWORK MUCH STRONGER

CROSS BRACING ON TOP OF A FRAMEWORK

FOLDS GIVE STRENGTH

PAPER TOWER

PAPER BRIDGE

CURVED FOLDS

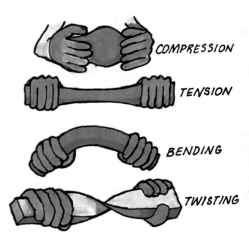

COMPRESSION

TENSION

BENDING

TWISTING

# Photography

Photography is a very valuable tool to the designer and communicator. The popular image of photography being easy, and something you don't have to think about, is·wrong. It may sell cameras but it won't make your photos any better. Get to know your camera, take some time in understanding how it works.

Plan a few shots in detail and make notes of what you expect to happen, then analyse the pictures when you get them back. In this way you can learn from your mistakes. Keep notes about all your pictures.

Decide what the purpose of the picture is, and then decide what it should have in it. Is it supposed to capture a mood or is it to record an object or a scene? Will someone want to examine it carefully or just want to flick through a series of your pictures to get an idea?

Plan a shooting sequence before you start taking pictures. This may be just a list or it could be quite detailed sketches.

Talk to experts and listen to what they say.

Work carefully, try and avoid being rushed.

Be **extra** careful loading and unloading films, and setting controls on the camera.

Always rehearse what you are going to do before you shoot it. Never try things out for the first time on an important shot.

A RECORD PHOTOGRAPH -TO SHOW A PARTICULAR SITUATION.

A RECORD PHOTOGRAPH - TO SHOW A PARTICULAR OBJECT.

A PHOTOGRAPH THAT IS DESIGNED TO SHOCK AND INFLUENCE PEOPLE.

A PHOTOGRAPH THAT SETS A CERTAIN MOOD OR FEELING.

Taking record shots of your work will save you having to store models and delicate things. Set up the objects so that they can easily be seen. Use a plain sheet of paper for a background; organise the lighting to avoid shadows and glaring reflections. Make sure your camera will focus on the object to give you as big an image as possible.

# Storyboards

Storyboards are used in many forms by professionals of the graphics industry. Their principle is that of reducing a process to a series of pictures or diagrams which sum up the action. The cartoon strip is a familiar form of storyboard, but you'll also find it used in cookery, DIY and gardening books.

It is a skill which requires you to look very carefully at what is happening and to pick out the pictures which tell the most. Practise by closely observing a TV commercial and write/draw a storyboard for it.

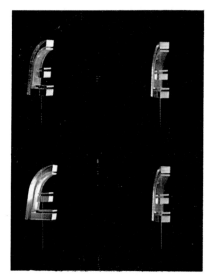

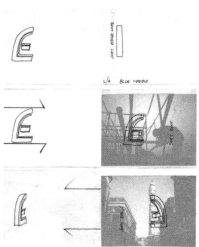

This storyboard was done for the opening titles of The Money Programme on BBC 2. It was produced along with a detailed shooting sequence which gave specific instructions to the animator. A storyboard not only helps to show the sequence of operations but also shows the kinds of pictures needed to describe them.

# Video and TV

If you have access to video and TV equipment, you will find it a valuable tool in all kinds of graphic work. It can provide nearly instant pictures of things. Sequences and processes can be recorded and analysed at length. Opinions and facts can be presented in an entertaining and visual way.

If what you are doing is more than just collecting information, you must decide who it is for and what effect you want it to have.

You should produce some kind of script or storyboard first. Because you are making a moving recording your instructions may have to include telling the camera operator what to do (like zoom in or pan left). You may also have to match the pictures to a script, which might be what people say in the video or may be a commentary added to the pictures later.

FROM YOUR 'STORYBOARD' WORK OUT YOUR SHOOTING INSTRUCTIONS.

COMPARE THE VIDEO AND YOUR STORYBOARD. DOES IT DO WHAT YOU WANTED?

Check your equipment carefully and also discuss your ideas with experts. Always rehearse your shots before you take them. Try to see the potential mistakes before you shoot scenes rather than afterwards. Don't underestimate how long it can take to get the simplest of things right.

# Packaging and Product Graphics

Collect different brands of the same item such as washing powder, toothpaste, soap or beans. Look at the way the package is made, how the words and images are used to describe the product, and then record what impression the different brands give you. Check your opinion with other people.

An interesting exercise is to take a product and try to design a series of packages and graphics all of which are different:

- one high class and up-market
- one cheap and cheerful
- one for children
- one healthy
- one for a certain supermarket chain.

Then fill them with an identical product, for example sugar, salt, rice, bread or muesli, and allow people to sample the product. Their different opinions will give you a feeling for the effect that the package has on the contents.

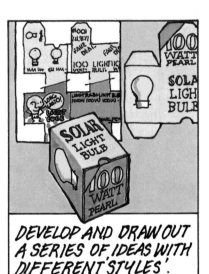

DEVELOP AND DRAW OUT A SERIES OF IDEAS WITH DIFFERENT 'STYLES'.

PEOPLE'S REACTIONS TO YOUR PRESENTATION AND IDEAS ARE IMPORTANT.

Remember that different parts of the graphics have to do different jobs. The logo and pack must be eye catching (will the product be seen singly or will there be lots of them on a shelf?) The words must be easy to read but not overpower the rest of the pack. Will there be bar codes or government warnings or trade marks or date stamps on the package? You'll have to consider all this.

# Simplified Plans

Any chart or map is an exercise in communication where what is important is chosen and what is not important is left out. The aim is to provide just enough information and not confuse the reader.

These different kinds of plan are for different users.

The most difficult decision is always how much to leave out, and how much information the user will be able to understand. A good technique for simplifying plans is to give a person verbal directions, to tape record this and then to construct your plan from this information.

AN AERIAL PHOTOGRAPH
·NO GRAPHIC DETAILS,
·QUITE COMPLICATED.

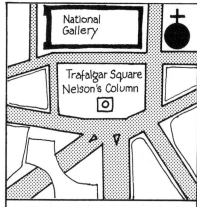

NOTICE WHAT HAS BEEN ADDED AND LEFT OUT TO MAKE THIS INTO A MAP.

WHO IS THIS MAP FOR? COMPARE THIS WITH THE AERIAL VIEW.

THIS MAP IS FOR A VERY SPECIFIC JOB. WHO IS IT FOR? WHAT DO THEY NEED?

WHO IS GOING TO USE YOUR MAP? WHAT INFORMATION WILL THEY NEED?

TEST OUT YOUR IDEAS BY ASKING SOMEONE TO TRY TO USE YOUR MAP.

Whilst these plans appear easy at first to design and are based on very simple ideas, they do need very careful work so that the simple idea is easy to understand. Always produce good quality first ideas and draw them out with care.

## References

# Typography

Typography is concerned with the shape of printed letters (typefaces) and the arrangement of the words on the page. In general all letter shapes give a certain mood, some are easier to read, and some are more decorative than others. It depends what you want – the purpose of the words on a soap packet is very different from that of a motorway sign, in terms of image and legibility. You have probably seen most of these letter shapes, and there are certain things that you will associate with them.

The letter shapes that are used in texts will often be different from those used for headings, road signs etc. In order to make reading matter easy to read, the designer will not only think about the shape and size of the letters, but also about the spaces between the letters, between the words, between the lines and the length of the lines. Compare the examples (right). Is one easier to read than the others? Why?

abcdefghijklmnopqrstuvwxyz
ABCDEFGHIJKLMNOPQRSTUVWXYZ

abcdefghijklmnopqrstuvwxyz
ABCDEFGHIJKLMNOPQRSTUVWXYZ

abcdefghijklmnopqrstuvwxyz
ABCDEFGHIJKLMNOPQRSTUVWXYZ

*abcdefghijklmnopqrstuvwxyz*
*ABCDEFGHIJKLMNOPQRSTUVWXYZ*

abcdefghijklmnopqrstuvwxyz
ABCDEFGHIJKLMNOPQRSTUVWXYZ

Collect your own examples of titles and text graphics. Note what impression they give and how easy to read they are.

This shows some of the stages it took to turn the typescript (centre) intro printed pages. The designer put instructions for the typesetters on a form (top left), such as the typeface (Rockwell), the size of the letters and amount of space between the lines (10/12½) and the length of the lines. It also shows layout sheets on to which the typeset text was pasted.

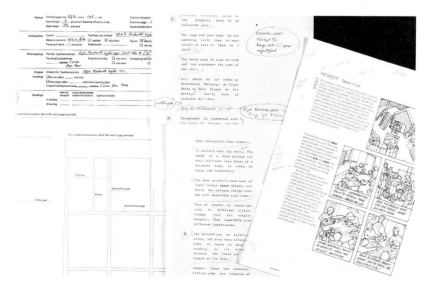

# Layout

The combination of the typography that you use and
the arrangement of the page is called the layout.
The layout of a page will affect the way it is used,
read, and the impression that it gives to the reader.

Before you start to work out the layout of a page
think:

- Who is it for?
- What does it have to do?
- What image do you want it to give?
- Do you have to write answers on it?
- How important is the information on it?

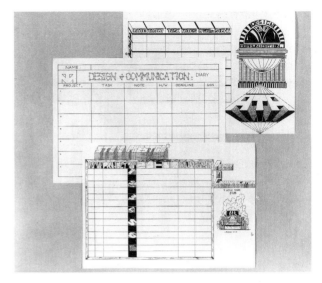

These two newspapers use
different layouts. What do you
think of the differences? What
impression do they give you?

The other examples show
three different layouts. Who are
they intended for? Why did the
designers choose these layouts?
Could you improve the layouts, or
do you think they are right as they
are?

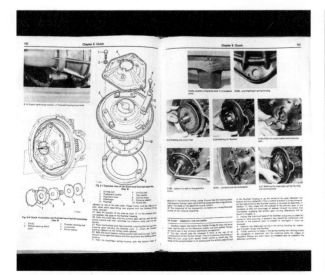

# Layout

These examples are all ways of presenting goods for people to buy. The layouts are very different. What are your impressions?

The listings is easy to read, cheap, and simple but it shows you nothing of the products.

The Argos catalogue shows you the products and tries to say that these are excellent, well-known products.

The Habitat catalogue says 'This is our style, when you buy one of our products you are buying a life-style.'

Do you agree with these opinions?

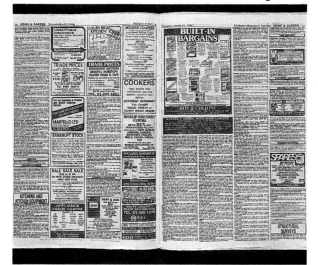

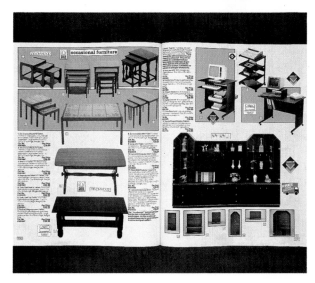

# Mechanisms

Study the mechanisms that you come across as you tackle your projects. When you take an object apart, make notes on its mechanism. The diagram on the right shows some basic mechanisms; you may come across others.

Mechanisms are one of the most difficult systems to understand and apply in a design project because you must be able to decide what the principle is and then convert that idea into a reality (mostly by seeing the object in your head).

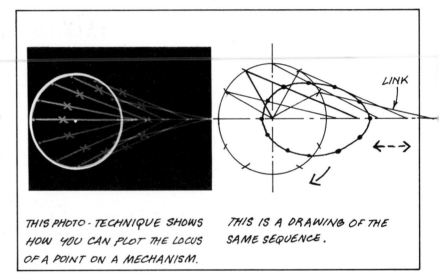

| BASIC LEVERS | $W \times D = w \times d$ |
| GEARS BELTS AND PULLEYS | $D:d$ IS THE GEAR RATIO |
| CAMS AND CRANKS | UP DOWN ROUND · ROTARY TO LINEAR |
| SCREW THREADS | LIKE USING A LONG WEDGE |

A locus is the path of a point obeying a mathematical law (usually as part of a mechanism). In drawing a locus you are slowing down the action into a series of 'still' pictures.

The photo shows the technique with a 'strobe' light and the drawing shows the same process in drawing form.

LINK

THIS PHOTO · TECHNIQUE SHOWS HOW YOU CAN PLOT THE LOCUS OF A POINT ON A MECHANISM.

THIS IS A DRAWING OF THE SAME SEQUENCE.

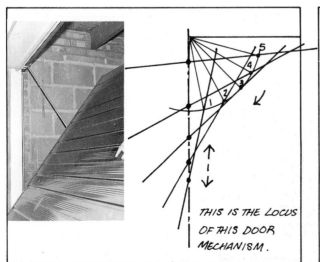

THIS IS THE LOCUS OF THIS DOOR MECHANISM.

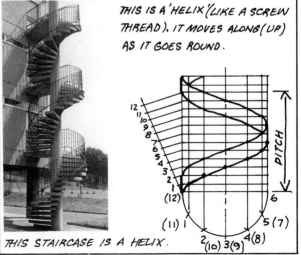

THIS IS A 'HELIX' (LIKE A SCREW THREAD). IT MOVES ALONG (UP) AS IT GOES ROUND.

PITCH

THIS STAIRCASE IS A HELIX.

# Graphs and Charts

Graphs and charts are ways of comparing and displaying information graphically so that it is easier to understand. There are generally accepted ways of doing graphs which seek to see mathematical relationships between the items being tested or displayed.

Histograms and pie charts are also ways of showing information to make it easier to understand.

Pictograms are even more pictorial and comprehensible.

Charts are excellent ways of recording and communicating processes, whether they just show a process or allow you to fill in parts of the process as you go along. The chart below is one that you might copy for plotting the topics you have covered throughout this course.

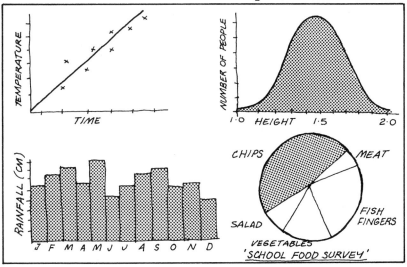

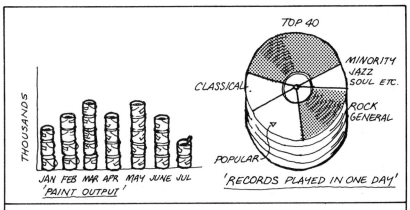

CHARTS AND DIAGRAMS SHOULD PRESENT INFORMATION IN WAYS THAT ARE ENTERTAINING AND EASY TO UNDERSTAND.

| | DESIGN | COMMUNICATION | MAKING | KNOWLEDGE | NOTES |
|---|---|---|---|---|---|
| PROJECT | | | | | |
| SELF EVALUATION SHEET/LOGO | o o | o o | o o | o | |
| SPACE TO LET | o o o | o o o | o o | o o | |
| MINI PROJECT PACKAGING | o o o o o o | o o o | o o o | o o o o | |
| PLAY STRUCTURE | o o o o o o | o o o o | o o o o | o o | |

THIS CHART IS OF A (GCSE) DESIGN AND COMMUNICATION COURSE. IT SHOWS WHICH OF THE PROJECTS HAVE COVERED WHICH TOPICS OF THE COURSE.

## References

# Geometry

**Drawing a 60 degree angle or equilateral triangle.** Draw an arc from a point along a line. With the same arc, mark along the first. Join the points. For 120 degrees repeat twice. See diagram A.

**Divide any angle into two.** Draw an arc any radius. Draw two arcs the same size to cross. Join the crossing point to the apex of the two lines. See B.

**Construct a perpendicular bisector.** This is a line at right angles to and half-way along the original line. Draw identical arcs to cross above and below the line. Join the crosses. See B.

**Division of a line into a certain number of parts.** Draw a line at an angle. Divide that line into the required number of pieces. Connect the last mark to the end of the line. Draw lines parallel to cut the original line. See C.

**Construct a hexagon on a given side.** Construct an equilateral triangle. With the same radius draw a circle. Mark off with the same radius around the circumference. See D.

**Construct a square.** Draw lines at 45 degrees from the end of the side. Draw a circle radius T. Mark off the side lengths around the circumference. Join the points with straight lines. See E.

**Construct a regular polygon (many sided figure) from a given side.** Find the centre of a circle for a hexagon.

Find the centre of a circle for a square.

The centre of the circle for a five-sided figure is midway between the two.

Seven, eight or nine sides are stepped up from this point. See F.

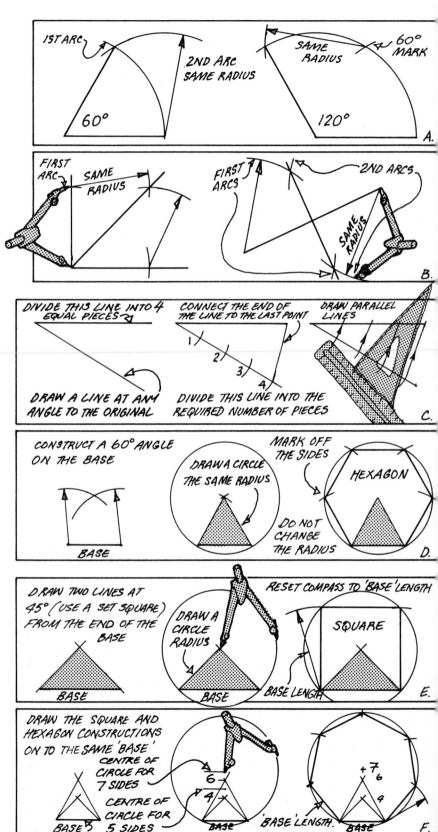

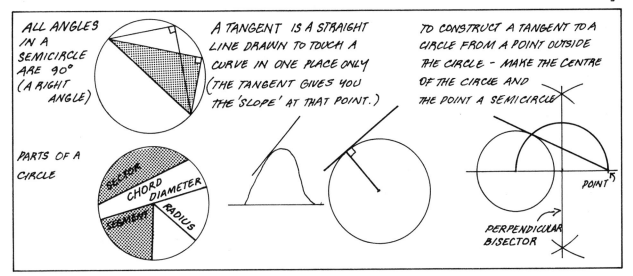

Imagine a circle rolling into a corner. Draw the path of the centre of the circle as it rolls down both sides. Where they cross is the centre of the corner radius. See G.

You may feel it necessary to practise these things. If you find you need them for your projects, invent a series of examples, then swap them with a friend and see if you can answer their questions.

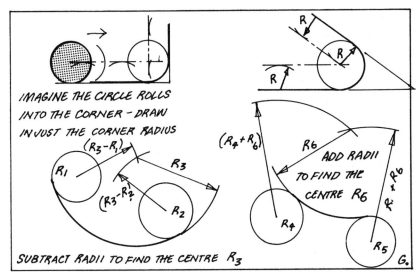

**Teachers' note** Geometry is the area where there is most variation between syllabuses. I have concentrated on the basic and central ideas. Please check your own syllabus to make sure of its particular requirements.

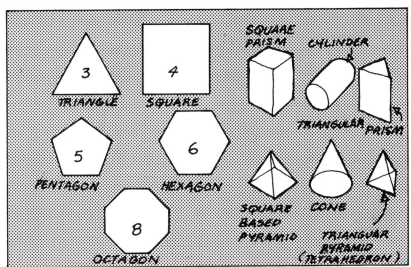

# True Length and Auxiliary views

Often, in order to show and simplify a particular detail, you need to draw an extra view of an object as well as front, side and plan views. This is called an auxiliary view. The way to construct it is to use the front, side and plan views and project the auxiliary view from them. Try to see the whole object and then think of turning it round to give the auxiliary view.

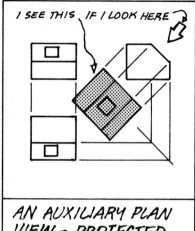

I SEE THIS  IF I LOOK HERE

AN AUXILIARY PLAN VIEW - PROJECTED FROM AN END VIEW.

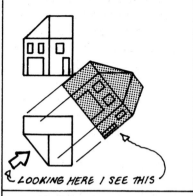

LOOKING HERE I SEE THIS

AN AUXILIARY SIDE VIEW - PROJECTED FROM A PLAN VIEW.

## True length principles

Often when using front, side and plan views you will draw edges and lines where the actual length of the lines are not shown. So that you can get the drawing right you need to know the true length of the edge. Look at these drawings of a ladder and a pyramid. The length of the side is sloping away in each view. The technique is to turn it around until what you are looking at is the true length.

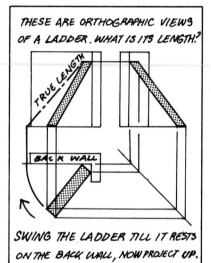

THESE ARE ORTHOGRAPHIC VIEWS OF A LADDER. WHAT IS ITS LENGTH?

TRUE LENGTH

BACK WALL

SWING THE LADDER TILL IT RESTS ON THE BACK WALL, NOW PROJECT UP.

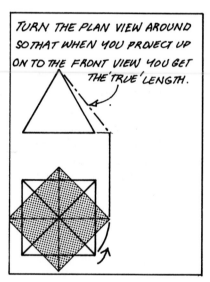

TURN THE PLAN VIEW AROUND SO THAT WHEN YOU PROJECT UP ON TO THE FRONT VIEW YOU GET THE 'TRUE' LENGTH.

## Drawing interpenetrations

Where solids or pipes join up you often need to work out the shape of the joining pieces so that they can be made. This is done by finding a true view, and projecting where the edges hit the other object. For circular objects (without edges) draw lines on the pipes and construct where they should be cut from the true view.

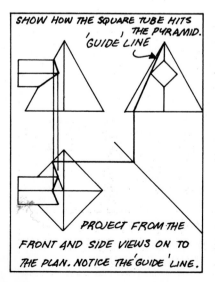

SHOW HOW THE SQUARE TUBE HITS THE PYRAMID.
'GUIDE' LINE

PROJECT FROM THE FRONT AND SIDE VIEWS ON TO THE PLAN. NOTICE THE 'GUIDE' LINE.

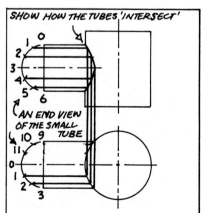

SHOW HOW THE TUBES 'INTERSECT'

AN END VIEW OF THE SMALL TUBE

THE SMALL TUBE IS DIVIDED INTO 12 EQUAL PIECES AND THEN THEIR INTERSECTION POINTS PLOTTED.

# Ergonomics and Anthropometrics

Ergonomics is to do with improving the design of machines and systems so that they are suitable for the people that use them. You should consider who the person is, whether they are big or small, old or young, strong or weak, etc.

- What do they have to do?
- Is it something that lasts a short or a long time?
- How much do they have to move about?
- Is what they do boring or interesting?
- Where will they be doing it? In extreme conditions, at home?
- Finally, and most importantly, what happens if they do it wrong? Is it dangerous to them and others?

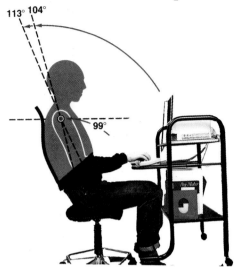

Anthropometrics is to do with the measurement of the human body. You can normally find the basic sizes and types of people on charts like this one. Take great care when you are using this sort of information because although a lot of people were tested to find the average sizes, this may not be average for the people you are considering. Always do a small survey of your own to check.

As important as the physical size of the users, is the range of things they have to do and how often the task has to be repeated. Make a careful record of what they have to do to complete the task and if there is a certain order that things have to be done in. How important is each of the stages? What happens if they get it wrong?

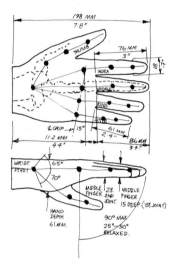

TEST YOUR DESIGN IDEAS WITH LIFE LIKE AND ACCURATE MODELS.

WATCH CAREFULLY THE WAY THAT PEOPLE USE YOUR DESIGNS.

## References

# Building Drawing

The techniques of representing buildings are exactly the same as those used for engineering drawing. Because buildings are bigger and therefore more complicated there are certain ways of representing things that are more diagramatic. The full range of symbols is in BS 1192 British Standards Association (Building Drawing Practice).

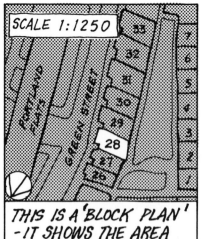

SCALE 1:1250

THIS IS A 'BLOCK PLAN' - IT SHOWS THE AREA AND THE SITE POSITION.

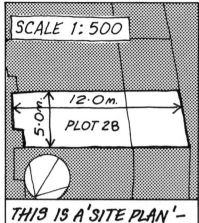

SCALE 1:500

THIS IS A 'SITE PLAN' - IT GIVES DETAILS OF THE SITE ON THE BLOCK PLAN.

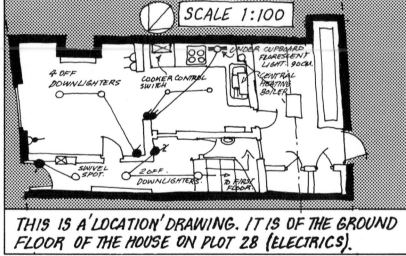

SCALE 1:100

THIS IS A 'LOCATION' DRAWING. IT IS OF THE GROUND FLOOR OF THE HOUSE ON PLOT 28 (ELECTRICS).

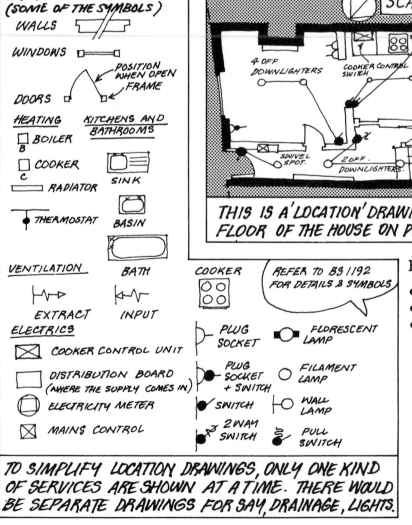

BUILDING DRAWINGS (SOME OF THE SYMBOLS)

WALLS

WINDOWS

POSITION WHEN OPEN
FRAME

DOORS

HEATING

KITCHENS AND BATHROOMS

BOILER B

COOKER C

RADIATOR

SINK

THERMOSTAT

BASIN

BATH

VENTILATION

EXTRACT

INPUT

COOKER

REFER TO BS 1192 FOR DETAILS & SYMBOLS

ELECTRICS

COOKER CONTROL UNIT

DISTRIBUTION BOARD (WHERE THE SUPPLY COMES IN)

ELECTRICITY METER

MAINS CONTROL

PLUG SOCKET

PLUG SOCKET + SWITCH

SWITCH

2 WAY SWITCH

FLORESCENT LAMP

FILAMENT LAMP

WALL LAMP

PULL SWITCH

TO SIMPLIFY LOCATION DRAWINGS, ONLY ONE KIND OF SERVICES ARE SHOWN AT A TIME. THERE WOULD BE SEPARATE DRAWINGS FOR SAY, DRAINAGE, LIGHTS.

## References

# Measurement

Throughout this course you will be asked to produce drawings of existing objects. You will need to measure them first. Always measure things carefully. Do not guess at the sizes. Check that you understand the ruler or equipment that you use. Is it in inches, millimetres, centimetres? Are the things you are writing down sensible or ten times too big?

**DIFFERENT OBJECTS WILL NEED DIFFERENT DEGREES OF ACCURACY.**

Depending on the object that you are measuring, differing degrees of accuracy may be needed. A building may be measured to within a centimetre, a garden to within ten centimetres or a watch to within one-hundredth of a millimetre. The kinds of equipment that you will need to measure various things will change depending on the accuracy that you need. Normally, complicated things are quite small, but what about an aeroplane?

**THINK ABOUT THE KINDS OF DRAWING YOU WILL NEED - SKETCH THE OBJECT.**

Think about the kinds of drawings you will need to produce for the object, Sketch the object in the way that you find easiest (perspective, orthographic or isometric sketches). Carefully add on the sizes as you measure them. It is a good idea to do this in pencil so that you can rub out or rearrange the dimensions as you take them.

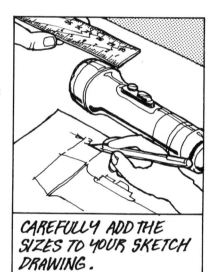

**CAREFULLY ADD THE SIZES TO YOUR SKETCH DRAWING.**

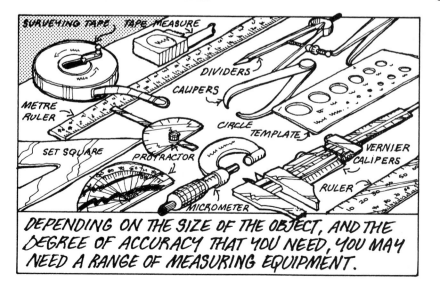

**DEPENDING ON THE SIZE OF THE OBJECT, AND THE DEGREE OF ACCURACY THAT YOU NEED, YOU MAY NEED A RANGE OF MEASURING EQUIPMENT.**

# Questionnaires and Testing

Collecting information can be difficult. First decide what things you need to know about. Make a list of them.

Look at the list and think about the best way to find out the things you need to know. For instance, if you need to know about the desk height for a particular office worker, do you ask the question 'Do you think your desk height is correct?'?

You may be better checking in an ergonomics book for the theoretical recommended height but also photographing the person at work and looking at the way they work or sit. Asking the question 'Do you get any physical problems because of your work?' may give you a better answer.

Don't ask questions that just give you yes/no answers or ones that lead the person to think you want a certain reply. The question 'You don't like your job, do you?' is likely to give you the answer 'No'!

Be aware that if you are trying to give a numerical answer, questioning small numbers of subjects may give you an inaccurate result. If you only ask questions of people who hold a certain viewpoint then you can prove anything you like. Try to make the sample either large, varied, or, even better, both.

Try to construct your interview or questionnaire so that the general questions are at the beginning. Make sure you say who you are and why you are asking questions. People can be quite defensive about giving information if they don't know how it will be used.

Be diplomatic and remember that if you are interviewing someone at work, they are not working while they are talking to you, so it might be sensible to ask permission from their supervisor.

If you have been interviewed by a professional you may find that they seem to repeat some of their questions, though using different words. This is to try and see if you are just saying the first thing that comes into your head or are really thinking about what you are saying.

Always be sure what you are going to do with the information that you collect and process. If you are looking for people's general feelings about something then just 'chatting around' the subject may give you a better answer. If you want to be able to say that a certain percentage of people are in favour of something then your questionnaire should be more structured.

Always try out your questionnaire on someone first to see which questions work. Did the people you asked understand what you wanted or should you say it in a different way? Would it be better to ask the questions in a different order?

## Testing and analysis of results

When you work on your projects you may need to carry out certain tests or to mock up your ideas and then get people to use objects you have made or talk about how they would use them. Design this as you would anything else. Decide what you need to know and what the best way of testing it is. Always be very careful and think things out before you start. Make the tests as real as you can. You don't want to put people off before they start by giving them the feeling that what they are being asked to do is a joke.

# Syllabus and Examinations

It is very important that your designing, making and communicating experience is as extensive as possible. This is the reason why the whole course should be based around a series of projects (as you would expect from a practical subject). It is also why you are encouraged to record what you are doing and what you have learned as you go along. Because all your work is important you are encouraged to present things well at each stage.

All the GCSE CDT: Design and Communication syllabuses have the same aims:

1. To help students gain experience and understanding through researching, planning, designing, making and testing.
2. To encourage learning so that practical and technological problems can be solved.
3. To develop skills in communication, layout, designing and making.
4. To encourage students to link their practical work to their own interests and abilities.
5. To encourage students to be thoughtful, to make choices and to work on their own.
6. To encourage in students an idea of technology and how it controls the world we live in.
7. To help students to make choices based on how things look, how they work, how much they cost and what value they are to people.
8. To enable students to use graphics and communicate ideas and information.
9. To enable students to think and communicate in three dimensions.
10. To enable students to design and communicate by thinking broadly, having lots of ideas, testing them and choosing the best ones for the particular job.

The skills that are covered by the course are split into three basic types:

- design skills
- subject-related skills
- knowledge skills.

Design skills include improving the things that you design by improving your way of reaching a solution.

Subject-related skills are all of those things you do which are about communication. What do you have to communicate? Who are you communicating to? Why do they need to be communicated with? You need to ask all of these questions. Also included are the skills you will need in order to make things.

Knowledge skills are the particular things that you need to know – from things which are basic principles that you can build on, to more general principles that show how the course relates to the outside world.

The whole course should be made up of these three headings:

| | | |
|---|---|---|
| Design skills | 40% | (around) |
| Subject-related skills | 35% | (around) |
| Knowledge | 25% | (around) |

Please check your own syllabus because there are differences between the exact percentages given by each examining board.

Your course will be split into three different parts and you will be assessed on each part:

1. Coursework – this is all the work that you do during the course. It is worth around 40 per cent of the marks.
2. A special design project which is given to you before the examinations, which you have about two months to work on in school. This project is sent away to be marked and is worth about 30 per cent. Through this project you will have the chance to show all the skills of designing, communicating, testing and making that you have learnt. The subject of the project is given to you by the exam board.
3. An examination which you do at the end of your course which is worth around 30 per cent.

Some syllabuses use the idea of 'mini projects'. A mini project could be any project suggested in this book, or one of your own choice. This will be worth about 15 per cent of the 40 per cent of your coursework marks. Your project will be assessed by you and your teacher and then at the end of the course a moderator (an expert from the exam board) will come and check the marking. A moderator's job is to make sure that the marks you have been given compare fairly with other schools, just in case you and your teacher have been too mean or too generous in your marking.

Your project will be given marks for the following areas:

1. You will have to show the ideas and stages you

went through as you thought about your project, such as your first ideas for possible solutions and notes on what you needed to know.

2. You will have to show that you can organise yourself to research extra information needed so that you can decide whether your ideas are sensible or not.

3. You will have to show that you can make things in a variety of materials such as paper, card, wood, plastic and Lego:
   - to test out your ideas,
   - to make up your chosen idea.

4. You will have to show that you can communicate ideas about graphics and objects in a variety of ways, depending on the reason for the drawing e.g. engineering drawings, assembly drawings, 3D sketches or design idea sketches.

5. You will have to show that you can test and judge your ideas in a variety of ways – drawings, models and the finished products. Also that you can judge at each stage what to do next and how to proceed.

6. You will have to show that you have worked hard and made an effort to do things as well as you can and to learn from your mistakes rather than be put off by them.

The written paper (called written even though most of the answers will be through drawings) is to test the things you have learnt during the course, specifically in the area that the syllabus calls knowledge and communication skills. It will be in two parts.

1. Several short questions asking for answers about small parts of the topics you have learnt.

2. Longer questions about larger areas of the course.

Sitting down and looking through your work as a way of revising for this course **does not work.** You must attempt trial questions. At first, time how long they take, but don't worry about spending too long on them. Finally, practise working at exam speed. When you are revising or taking the exam, remember the following points:

1. Read the questions **very** carefully. Underline the **key words** as you read them so that you *don't* misunderstand anything.

2. Identify what things you need to know to answer the questions and work out what things the examiners are looking for so that they can give you marks. (Look at the specimen question opposite.)

Plan out your revision, start to plan well in advance and give yourself a daily time table saying not only what subject you are going to study but which area and which part within that area.
- Don't spend more than half an hour concentrating without a short break.
- Vary the revision you do in subjects and topics.
- Don't leave the same subject until last every time or your revision on it will be poor.
- Revise a topic one day, test yourself three days later and revise a bit extra, then test yourself again in seven days.

Don't panic about written exams. **Before** you go into the exam room you should know

1. What percentage of the marks this part of the exam is worth. It will be between 30 and 40 per cent of the total exam (not 100 per cent).

2. How many marks are given for each section. On many of the exams it will say how many marks for each question.

Remember, it is better to attempt all questions (even if you only get half the marks on some) rather than only attempt a few of the questions but try to get full marks on them.

7　Project a section on **X – X** of the plastic moulding. [6]

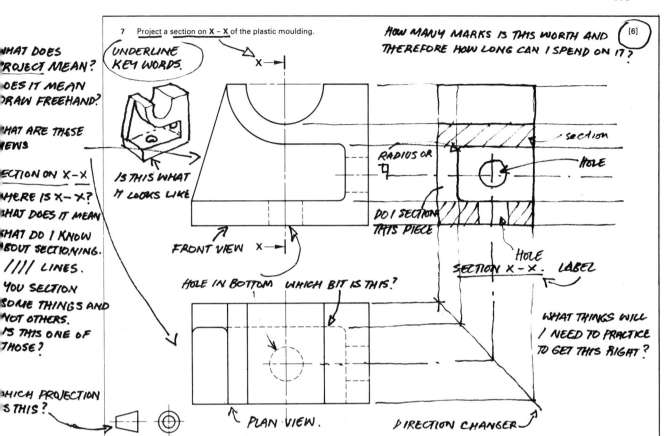

Handwritten annotations:

UNDERLINE KEY WORDS.

HOW MANY MARKS IS THIS WORTH AND THEREFORE HOW LONG CAN I SPEND ON IT?

WHAT DOES PROJECT MEAN?

DOES IT MEAN DRAW FREEHAND?

WHAT ARE THESE VIEWS

SECTION ON X – X

WHERE IS X – X?

WHAT DOES IT MEAN

WHAT DO I KNOW ABOUT SECTIONING.

//// LINES.

YOU SECTION SOME THINGS AND NOT OTHERS.

IS THIS ONE OF THOSE?

WHICH PROJECTION IS THIS?

IS THIS WHAT IT LOOKS LIKE

FRONT VIEW　X

HOLE IN BOTTOM　WHICH BIT IS THIS?

PLAN VIEW.

RADIUS OR

DO I SECTION THIS PIECE

section

HOLE

HOLE

SECTION X – X　LABEL

WHAT THINGS WILL I NEED TO PRACTICE TO GET THIS RIGHT?

DIRECTION CHANGER

# Index

£8·70

# DESIGN

Longman

Longman Group UK Limited,
*Longman House, Burnt Mill, Harlow,
Essex CM20 2JE, England ·
and Associated Companies throughout the world.*

First published 1989
Set in Linotron 10/12.5 point Rockwell

Produced by Longman Group (FE) Ltd
Printed in Hong Kong

ISBN 0 582 00270 2

## Acknowledgements

The author would like to thank the following very much for
their help: the students at Islington Sixth-Form Centre;
David Stone and Islington School's Environmental Project;
Greenpeace; CEGB; Phill Rooke; Jo Compton; Ken
Lumsden of Conran Associates; Alan Colville of Ian Logan
Designs; Adrian Stokes, David Banham and Stuart Lambert
of ASA; Richard Miles of F & M; Jon Isherwood and Tony
Whitehead of Isherwood and Co; Malcolm Hird of Islington
Sixth-Form Centre for Computer Graphics; Peter Campbell
for Energy; Chetz Colwell and Maeve Dorian for Notes;
Pete Hawksby for Photography; Ricky Beech of Islington
Green School, and Arnold Roberts for Electronics.
The publishers are grateful to the following for permission
to reproduce photographs and other copyright material:
Ace Photo Agency, pp. 81 *centre* (photo: Gabe Palmer), 88
*above left* (photo: Roger Howard); Aerofilms, p. 92 *above
left*; Argos, p. 95 *centre*; Barnabys Picture Library, p. 96
*below right*; J. Allan Cash, p. 87; CEGB, p. 34; Exchange &
Mart, p. 95 *above*; Geographers A-Z Map Co. Ltd, p. 92
*below left*; Edward Gorey, *The Dwindling Party*,
Heinemann, p. 94 *below right* (below inset); Sally &
Richard Greenhill, pp. 72 *above* (inset on collage), 88
*centre left*, 88 *centre right*; *The Guardian*, p. 94 *centre
right*; Habitat, p. 95 *below*; Haynes Manual, p. 94 *below
left*; London Regional Transport, p. 92 *below right*; Jan
Pienkowski, *Gossip*, Gallery Five, p. 94 *below right* (above
inset); *Today* Newspaper, p. 94 *centre left*.

We are unable to trace the copyright holder of the
following and would be grateful for any information to
enable us to do so: p. 89 *below*.